Splunk 7 Essentials
Third Edition

Demystify machine data by leveraging datasets, building reports, and sharing powerful insights

J-P Contreras
Erickson Delgado
Betsy Page Sigman

BIRMINGHAM - MUMBAI

MW00452348

Splunk 7 Essentials
Third Edition

Commissioning Editor: Sunith Shetty
Acquisition Editor: Vinay Argekar
Content Development Editor: Mayur Pawanikar
Technical Editor: Sagar Sawant
Copy Editors: Vikrant Phadke, Safis Editing
Project Coordinator: Nidhi Joshi
Proofreader: Safis Editing
Indexer: Rekha Nair
Graphics: Tania Dutta
Production Coordinator: Arvindkumar Gupta

First published: February 2015
Second edition: September 2016
Third edition: March 2018

Production reference: 1270318

Published by Packt Publishing Ltd.
Livery Place
35 Livery Street
Birmingham
B3 2PB, UK.

ISBN 978-1-78883-911-2

www.packtpub.com

`mapt.io`

Mapt is an online digital library that gives you full access to over 5,000 books and videos, as well as industry leading tools to help you plan your personal development and advance your career. For more information, please visit our website.

Why subscribe?

- Spend less time learning and more time coding with practical eBooks and Videos from over 4,000 industry professionals

- Improve your learning with Skill Plans built especially for you

- Get a free eBook or video every month

- Mapt is fully searchable

- Copy and paste, print, and bookmark content

PacktPub.com

Did you know that Packt offers eBook versions of every book published, with PDF and ePub files available? You can upgrade to the eBook version at `www.PacktPub.com` and as a print book customer, you are entitled to a discount on the eBook copy. Get in touch with us at `service@packtpub.com` for more details.

At `www.PacktPub.com`, you can also read a collection of free technical articles, sign up for a range of free newsletters, and receive exclusive discounts and offers on Packt books and eBooks.

Contributors

About the author

J-P Contreras, a Splunk-certified administrator and sales engineer, has delivered value-oriented data analytics and performance planning solutions for 20+ years. He has built award-winning consulting teams to help companies turn data into analytical insights. He helps companies implement Splunk and enjoys everything the Splunk community offers. He received his MBA in e-commerce from DePaul University's Kellstadt Graduate School of Business, Chicago, in 2001. He trains in DePaul's Continuing Education Program and is a member of DePaul's Driehaus School of Business Advisory Board.

> *I'd like to thank my family, especially my wife and children and my close friends for making life so enjoyable.*
>
> *I'd also like to extend my gratitude to Steve Koelpin. Steve is a certified Splunk consultant and a member of SplunkTrust. His "Tips from the Fez" commentary which you will find in the book to provides additional context to points presented. I thank Steve for his partnership and friendship.*

Erickson Delgado is an enterprise architect who loves to mine and analyze data. He began using Splunk in version 4.0 and has pioneered its use into his current work. He has worked with start-up companies in the Philippines to help build their open source infrastructure. He has developed applications with Python and node.js and is interested in Go and recovering programming with C/C++. In the recent years, he engaged himself in employing DevOps in his work.

He blows off steam by saltwater fishing, mountain biking, crafting robots, and touring the country. He lives in Orlando.

Betsy Page Sigman is a distinguished professor at the McDonough School of Business at Georgetown University in Washington, D.C. She has taught courses in statistics, project management, databases, and electronic commerce for the last 16 years, and has been recognized with awards for teaching and service. She has also worked at George Mason University in the past. Her recent publications include a Harvard Business case study and a Harvard Business review article. Additionally, she is a frequent media commentator on technological issues and big data.

About the reviewers

Dmitry Anoshin is a technologist and expert in building and implementing big data and analytics solutions, with a successful track record of business/digital intelligence projects in many industries, such as retail, finance, marketing, machine tools, and e-commerce. He has in-depth knowledge of BI, ETL, data warehousing, data modeling, and big data. He is proficient in data integration and many data warehousing methodologies.

He has completed many multinational full BI/DI life cycle projects. He also has a background in multiple relational databases, OLAP systems, and NoSQL.

Ruben Oliva Ramos is an engineer with a master's in computer and electronic engineering and specialization in teleinformatics and networking from University of Salle Bajio in Leon, Mexico. He has 5+ years of experience of building web applications to control and monitor devices linked to Arduino and Raspberry Pi.
He teaches mechatronics, electronics, robotics, automation, and microcontrollers. He is a consultant and developer for projects in control and monitoring systems and datalogger data using Android, iOS, HTML5, ASP.NET, databases, web servers, and hardware programming.

Packt is searching for authors like you

If you're interested in becoming an author for Packt, please visit `authors.packtpub.com` and apply today. We have worked with thousands of developers and tech professionals, just like you, to help them share their insight with the global tech community. You can make a general application, apply for a specific hot topic that we are recruiting an author for, or submit your own idea.

Table of Contents

Preface

Splunk is a search, reporting, and analytics software platform for machine data. More organizations than ever are adopting Splunk to make informed decisions in such areas as IT operations, information security, and the **Internet of Things (IoT)**.

This book is for anyone who needs to get reports and analytics from machine data. The first two chapters of the book will quickly get you started with a simple Splunk installation and the setup of a sample machine data generator called **Eventgen**. You will then learn about searching machine data and enriching it with additional fields to provide analytical value. After this, you will learn to create various reports, dashboards, and alerts. You will also explore Splunk's Pivot functionality to model data for business users, who can then create visualizations with point-and-click ease.

You will also have the opportunity to test drive Splunk's powerful HTTP event collector. After covering the core Splunk functionality, you'll be provided with some real-world best practices in using Splunk and information on how to build upon what you've learned in this book to take Splunk to your organization.

Throughout the book, there will be additional comments and best practice recommendations from a member of the SplunkTrust community, called **Tips from the Fez**.

Who this book is for

This book is for the beginners who want to get well versed in the services offered by Splunk 7. If you want to be a data/business analyst or a system administrator, this book is what you need. No prior knowledge of Splunk is required.

What this book covers

Chapter 1, *Splunk – Getting Started*, covers concepts to extend Splunk to your organization. We cover the vast Splunk community and online ecosystem.

Chapter 2, *Bringing in Data*, teaches essential concepts such as forwarders, indexes, events, event types, fields, sources, and sourcetypes.

Chapter 3, *Search Processing Language*, covers more about using search and other commands to analyze your data.

Chapter 4, *Reporting, Alerts, and Search Optimization*, shows how to classify your data using Event Types, enrich it using Lookups, and normalize it using Tags.

Chapter 5, *Dynamic Dashboarding*, creates a fully functional form-based dashboard that will allow you to change the inputs and affect the dashboard data by using tokens and assigning them to search panels.

Chapter 6, *Data Models and Pivot*, uses a very intuitive Pivot editor to create three different visualizations: area chart, pie chart, and single value with a trend sparkline.

Chapter 7, *HTTP Event Collector*, discusses **HTTP event collector (HEC)** and how it can be used to send data directly from an application to Splunk.

Chapter 8, *Best Practices and Advanced Queries*, introduces a few extra skills that will help make you a powerful Splunker.

Chapter 9, *Taking Splunk to the Organization*, concludes our book with thoughts, concepts, and ideas to take this new knowledge ahead and apply to an organization.

To get the most out of this book

To start with the book, you will first need to download Splunk from https://www.splunk.com/en_us/download.html.

You can find the official installation manual at http://docs.splunk.com/Documentation/Splunk/latest/Installation/Systemrequirements.

Download the example code files

You can download the example code files for this book from your account at www.packtpub.com. If you purchased this book elsewhere, you can visit www.packtpub.com/support and register to have the files emailed directly to you.

You can download the code files by following these steps:

1. Log in or register at www.packtpub.com.
2. Select the **SUPPORT** tab.
3. Click on **Code Downloads & Errata**.
4. Enter the name of the book in the **Search** box and follow the onscreen instructions.

Once the file is downloaded, please make sure that you unzip or extract the folder using the latest version of:

- WinRAR/7-Zip for Windows
- Zipeg/iZip/UnRarX for Mac
- 7-Zip/PeaZip for Linux

The code bundle for the book is also hosted on GitHub at https://github.com/PacktPublishing/Splunk-7-Essentials-Third-Edition. We also have other code bundles from our rich catalog of books and videos available at https://github.com/PacktPublishing/. Check them out!

Download the color images

We also provide a PDF file that has color images of the screenshots/diagrams used in this book. You can download it here: http://www.packtpub.com/sites/default/files/downloads/Splunk7EssentialsThirdEdition_ColorImages.pdf.

Conventions used

There are a number of text conventions used throughout this book.

CodeInText: Indicates code words in text, database table names, folder names, filenames, file extensions, pathnames, dummy URLs, user input, and Twitter handles. Here is an example: "You can either do it using the following icacls command or change it using the Windows GUI"

A block of code is set as follows:

```
SPL> index=main earliest=-1h latest=now | stats
count(eval(if(http_status_code < "400", 1, NULL))) AS successful_requests
count(eval(if(http_status_code >= "400", 1, NULL))) AS
unsuccessful_requests by http_status_code
```

When we wish to draw your attention to a particular part of a code block, the relevant lines or items are set in bold:

```
016-07-21 23:58:50:227303,96.32.0.0,GET,/destination/LAX/details,-,80,
-,10.2.1.33,Mozilla/5.0 (Macintosh; Intel Mac OS X 10_8_5)
AppleWebKit/537.36 (KHTML; like Gecko) Chrome/29.0.1547.76
Safari/537.36,500,0,0,823,3053
```

Any command-line input or output is written as follows:

```
Windows: C:> dir C:\Splunk\etc\apps\SA-Eventgen
Linux: ls -l /$SPLUNK_HOME/etc/apps/
```

Bold: Indicates a new term, an important word, or words that you see onscreen. For example, words in menus or dialog boxes appear in the text like this. Here is an example: "On the **Server controls** page, click on the **Restart Splunk** button. Click on **OK** when asked to confirm the restart."

 Warnings or important notes appear like this.

 Tips and tricks appear like this.

Get in touch

Feedback from our readers is always welcome.

General feedback: Email feedback@packtpub.com and mention the book title in the subject of your message. If you have questions about any aspect of this book, please email us at questions@packtpub.com.

Errata: Although we have taken every care to ensure the accuracy of our content, mistakes do happen. If you have found a mistake in this book, we would be grateful if you would report this to us. Please visit www.packtpub.com/submit-errata, selecting your book, clicking on the Errata Submission Form link, and entering the details.

Piracy: If you come across any illegal copies of our works in any form on the Internet, we would be grateful if you would provide us with the location address or website name. Please contact us at copyright@packtpub.com with a link to the material.

If you are interested in becoming an author: If there is a topic that you have expertise in and you are interested in either writing or contributing to a book, please visit authors.packtpub.com.

Reviews

Please leave a review. Once you have read and used this book, why not leave a review on the site that you purchased it from? Potential readers can then see and use your unbiased opinion to make purchase decisions, we at Packt can understand what you think about our products, and our authors can see your feedback on their book. Thank you!

For more information about Packt, please visit packtpub.com.

Splunk – Getting Started
1

Splunk is a multinational software company that offers its core platform, Splunk Enterprise, as well as many related offerings built on the Splunk platform. Cofounded by Michael Baum, Rob Das, and Erik Swan, Splunk's name was inspired by the process of exploring caves, or spelunking. The Splunk platform helps a wide variety of organizational personas, such as analysts, operators, developers, testers, managers, and executives. They get analytical insights from machine-created data. Splunk collects, stores, and provides powerful analytical capabilities, enabling organizations to act on often powerful insights derived from this data.

The Splunk Enterprise platform was built with IT operations in mind. When companies had IT infrastructure problems, troubleshooting and solving problems was immensely difficult, complicated, and manual. Splunk was built to collect and make log files from IT systems searchable and accessible. Splunk is commonly used for information security and development operations, as well as more advanced use cases for custom machines, Internet of Things, and mobile devices.

 Throughout the book, we will be covering the fundamental concepts of Splunk so that you can learn quickly and efficiently. As the concepts become more complex, we reserve their deep discussion for Splunk's online documentation or the vibrant Splunk online community at http://docs.splunk.com. Wherever necessary, we provide links to help provide you with the practical skills and examples so that you can get started quickly.

With very little time, you can achieve direct results using Splunk, which you can access through a free enterprise trial license. While this license limits you to 500 MB of data ingested per day, it will allow you to quickly get up to speed with Splunk and learn the essentials of this powerful software.

If you follow what we've written closely, we believe you will quickly learn the fundamentals you need to use Splunk effectively. Together, we will make the most of the trial license and give you a visible result that you can use to create valuable insights for your company.

Towards the end of the book, we will cover concepts to extend Splunk to your organization, and cover the vast Splunk community and online ecosystem.

Tip from the Fez: Splunk sponsors a community known as **Splunk Trust**. Splunk Trust is made up of bright Splunk minds from around the world, who actively and successfully participate in the Splunk community, especially through the Splunk answers online site. A logo associated with this community is based on the historical headdress and named after the city of Fez, Morocco. Many fraternal organizations have adopted the use of a Fez, most notably in the United States by the Shriners organization. Throughout this book, we will tap into one of Splunk Trust's members to provide some additional best practice recommendations.

Your Splunk account

First, you will need to register for a Splunk account; go to `https://www.splunk.com/`. This is the account that you will use if you decide to purchase a license later. Go ahead and do this now. From here on, the password you use for your Splunk account will be referred to as your Splunk password.

Obtaining a Splunk account

To obtain your Splunk account, perform the following steps:

1. Go to the Splunk sign up page at `http://www.splunk.com`.
2. In the upper-right corner, click on the **Free Splunk** button.
3. Enter the information requested.
4. Create a username and password.
5. You will be taken to the Splunk download page, where you will need to click on the **Free Download** button under Splunk Enterprise as shown in the following screenshot:

Core Products

Splunk Enterprise
Software

✔ Unlimited users
✔ Unlimited data
✔ Collect and index any data
✔ Real-time search, analysis, and visualization
✔ Monitor and alert
✔ Mission-critical performance, scale, and reliability
✔ Splunk Premium Solutions and Apps from Splunkbase

⬇ Free Download

Splunk Cloud
Cloud Service

✔ Unlimited users
✔ Unlimited data
✔ Collect and index any data
✔ Real-time search, analysis, and visualization
✔ Monitor and alert
✔ Mission-critical performance, scale, and reliability — 100% uptime SLA
✔ Select Splunk Premium Solutions and Apps from Splunkbase

☁ Free Cloud Trial

6. You will then need to download the Splunk Enterprise software. Go to `http://download.splunk.com` and select the Splunk Enterprise free download. Choose your operating system, being careful to select 32 or 64-bit (whichever is appropriate in your case; most should select 64-bit, which most computers of today use). For Windows, download the `*.msi` file. For Linux, download the `*.tgz` file. In this book, we work with version 7.0.1.

The installation is very straightforward. Follow the steps for your particular operating system, whether it is Windows or Linux.

 This book assumes a single Splunk standalone installation. Make sure that there is no previous installation of Splunk in your system. If there is any, uninstall the prior version before proceeding with the next steps.

Installing Splunk on Windows

These are the instructions you need to follow to install Splunk on your Windows desktop. Take your time and do not rush the installation. Many chapters in this book will rely on these steps:

1. Run the installer that you downloaded.
2. Check the box to accept the License Agreement and then click on **Customize Options**, as shown in the following screenshot:

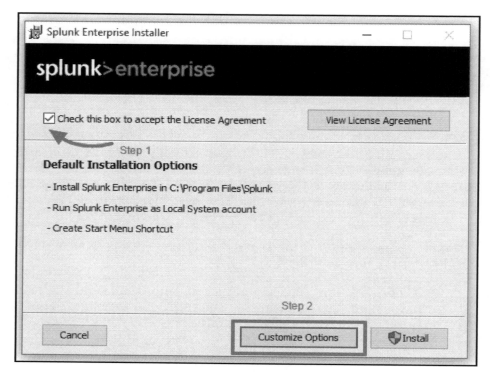

3. Change the installation path to C:\Splunk\. You will thank us later as it simplifies issuing **Splunk CLI (command line interface)** commands. This is also a best practice used by modern Windows administrators. Remember to eliminate white spaces in directory names as well, as it causes complications with scripting. Click on **Next** to continue, as seen in this screenshot:

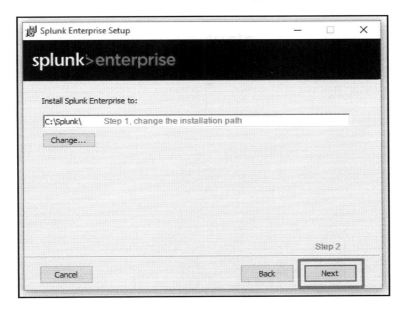

4. Install Splunk Enterprise as **Local System** and then click on **Next**.
5. Leave the checkbox selected to **Create Start Menu Shortcut**.
6. Click on **Install**.
7. Wait for the installation to complete.
8. Click on **Finish** to complete the installation. It will attempt to launch Splunk for the first time in your default browser.

 Throughout the book, you will see references to $SPLUNK_HOME. This will be the installation directory of Splunk. In Windows, as a convention used in this book, $SPLUNK_HOME will be at C:\Splunk\.

 For the Linux convention used in this book, $SPLUNK_HOME is where Splunk is installed in the particular user's home directory. Large-scale Splunk deployments should and will deviate from these personalized settings.

Installing Splunk on Linux

If you choose to install Splunk on a Linux machine, these are the instructions you need to follow. Take your time and do not rush the installation. For this Linux installation, the steps assume you will run Splunk in your user profile's home directory:

1. Decompress the `.tgz` file you downloaded. The result of the decompression is a `splunk` folder and all the related Splunk files contained inside.
2. Change the working directory to `$SPLUNK_HOME/bin`.
3. Run the following command to start Splunk for the first time:

   ```
   ./splunk start
   ```

4. Accept the Splunk license when prompted.
5. Splunk will start successfully and the end results should appear like this:

```
Starting splunk server daemon (splunkd)...
Done
                                                        [ OK ]

Waiting for web server at http://127.0.0.1:8000 to be available..... Done

If you get stuck, we're here to help.
Look for answers here: http://docs.splunk.com

The Splunk web interface is at http://linux4splunk:8000

[jp@linux4splunk bin]$
```

Tip from the Fez: In most organizational environments, it is common to install Splunk in `/opt/`. When installing on Linux, it is best practice to adjust the ulimit settings and disable transparent hugh page functionality for Splunk applications that will be loading data in real time, supporting a community of users.

Tip from the Fez: Unlike Windows installations, Splunk Linux installations aren't automatically configured to start upon reboot of the Splunk server. Ensure that you configure your Splunk instance on Linux for what is known as **boot start** so that if the Linux instance is restarted, Splunk will automatically restart with the operating system.

Tip from the Fez: In an enterprise environment, create a Linux user specifically for running Splunk and use that. Do not run Splunk as the Linux root user or an individuals user.

Logging in for the first time

Launch the application for the first time in your default browser. You can also manually access the Splunk web page via the `http://localhost:8000` URL if you have installed locally. If using a cloud instance, use `http://ipaddress:8000` since you are connecting via a traditional internet connection as opposed to locally.

 Splunk requires you to use a modern browser. It supports most versions of Google Chrome, Firefox, and newer versions of Internet Explorer. It may not support older versions of Internet Explorer.

Log in with the default username as **admin** and password as **changeme**, as indicated in the following screenshot:

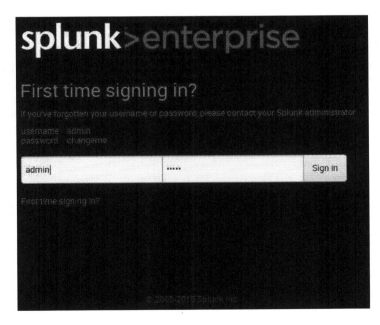

The next step is to change the default administrator password, while keeping the default username. **Do not skip** this step. Make security an integral part of your day-to-day routine. Choose a password that will be secure.

Assuming that all goes well, you will now see the default Splunk Enterprise landing page as follows:

Running a simple search

You are ready to run your first Splunk search:

1. Click directly on the green **Search & Reporting** app button. In this example, you use Splunk's very own internal index; this is Splunk's way of splunking itself (or collecting detailed information on all its underlying processes).

 An index is the term given to where Splunk stores event data captured from log files, APIs, HTTP events, delimited files, and other machine data sources. It is in some ways like a database, but should not be compared to traditional relational databases in functionality or performance.

2. In the **New Search** input, type in the following search query (more about the **Search Processing Language** (**SPL**) in Chapter 3, *Search Processing Language*):

```
SPL> index=_internal sourcetype=splunkd
```

The SPL> prefix will be used as a convention in this book to indicate a Splunk Search command. Since SPL is submitted via the Splunk user interface, there is no difference whether operating in Windows or Linux environments. The underscore before the index name _internal means that it is a system index internally used by Splunk. Omitting the underscore will not yield any result, as internal is not a default index.

3. This search query will have as an output the raw events from the metrics.log file that is stored in the _internal index. A log file keeps track of every event that takes place in the system. The _internal index keeps track of every event that occurs and makes it easily accessible.

4. Take a look at these raw events, as shown in the following screenshot. You will see fields listed on the left side of the screen. The important **Selected Fields** are **host**, **source**, and **sourcetype**. We will go into more detail about these later, but suffice to say that you will frequently search on one of these, as we have done here. As you can see from the highlighted fields, we indicated that we were looking for events where sourcetype=splunkd. Underneath **Selected Fields**, you will see **Interesting Fields**. As you can tell, the purposes of many of these fields are easy to guess as seen in the following screenshot:

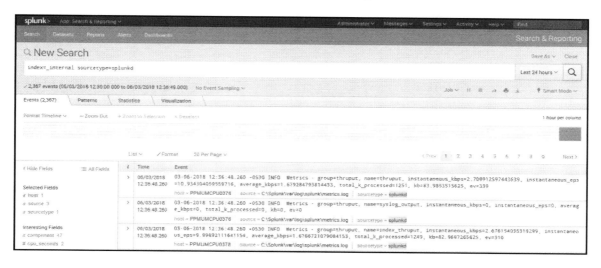

Creating a Splunk app

It is good practice to create a custom Splunk app to isolate the configurations you add to Splunk. You may never have created an app before, but you will quickly see it is not very difficult. Here, we will create a basic app called **Destinations** that we will use throughout this book:

1. Let's access the **Manage Apps** page. There are two ways to do this; you can either click on the **Apps** icon at the home page as shown in the following screenshot:

2. Or, select **Manage Apps** from the app dropdown in the top navigation bar of the **Search & Reporting** app:

3. At the **Manage Apps** page, click on the **Create app** icon shown in the following screenshot:

4. Finally, populate the forms with the following information to complete app creation. When you are done, click on the **Save** button to create your first Splunk app:

5. You have just created your very first Splunk app. Notice that it now appears in the list of apps and it has a status of **Enabled**, meaning it is ready to be used:

Name ⬍	Folder name ⬍	Version ⬍	Update checking ⬍	Visible ⬍	Sharing ⬍
SA-Eventgen	SA-Eventgen	@build.version@	Yes	Yes	Global	Permissions
SplunkForwarder	SplunkForwarder		Yes	No	App	Permissions
SplunkLightForwarder	SplunkLightForwarder		Yes	No	App	Permissions
Log Event Alert Action	alert_logevent	7.0.2	Yes	No	App	Permissions
Webhook Alert Action	alert_webhook	7.0.2	Yes	No	App	Permissions
Apps Browser	appsbrowser	7.0.2	Yes	No	App	Permissions
Destinations	destinations	1.0	Yes	Yes	App	Permissions
framework	framework		Yes	No	App	Permissions
Getting started	gettingstarted	1.0	Yes	Yes	App	Permissions

We will use this app to complete the exercises in this book, but first we need to make a few important changes:

1. Click on the **Permissions** link shown in the preceding screenshot
2. In the next window, under the **Sharing for config file-only objects** section, select **All apps**

These steps will ensure that the application will be accessible to the Eventgen add-on, which will be installed later in the chapter. Use the following screenshot as a guide:

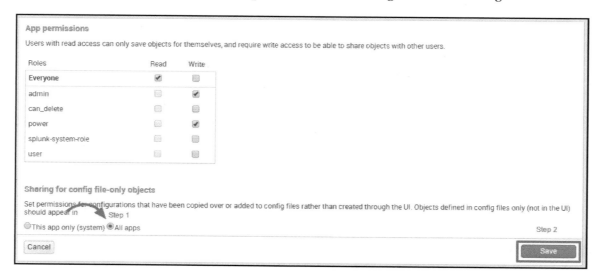

Splunk permissions are always composed of three columns: **Roles**, **Read**, and **Write**. A role refers to certain authorizations or permissions that can be taken on by a user. Selecting **Read** for a particular role grants the set of users in the role permission to view the object. Selecting **Write** will allow the set of users to modify the object. In the preceding screenshot, everyone (all users) will have access to view the **Destinations** app, but only the admin (you) and a power user can modify it.

Populating data with Eventgen

Machine data is produced by the many functions carried out by computers and other mechanical machines. If you work in an environment that is rich in machine data, you will most likely have many sources of readily available data inputs for Splunk. However, to facilitate learning in this book, we will use a Splunk add-on called the **Splunk Eventgen** to easily build real-time and randomized web log data. This is the type of data that would be produced by a web-based e-commerce company.

 If you need more detailed information about Eventgen, you can follow the project's GitHub repository at `https://github.com/splunk/eventgen/`.

Using the CLI to configure Eventgen

Here's an important tip for Windows users. Make it a habit to always launch your Command Prompt in administrator mode. This allows you to use commands that are unhindered by Windows security:

1. Right-click on the Windows start menu icon and select **Search**. In Windows 7, you can click on the Windows icon and the search window will be directly above it. In Windows 10, there is a search bar named **Cortana** next to the Windows icon that you can type into. They both have the same underlying function.
2. In the search bar, type `cmd`.
3. In the search results, look for `command.exe` (Windows 7) or Command Prompt (Windows 10), right-click on it, and then select **Run as administrator**.

Familiarize yourself with this step. Throughout the rest of the book, you will be frequently asked to open Command Prompt in administrator mode. You will know if you are in administrator mode, as it will say **administrator: Command Prompt** in the title of the Command Prompt window.

Installing the Eventgen add-on (Windows and Linux)

A Splunk add-on extends and enhances the base functionality of Splunk. An add-on typically enriches data using prebuilt rules for a specific source to enable faster analysis. In this section, you will be installing your first add-on, called **Splunk Eventgen**, which will help us pre-populate Splunk with real-time simulated web data:

1. Download the ZIP file from the Eventgen public repository, http://github.com/splunk/eventgen. Click on the green **Clone or download** button. For Linux users, we've placed a copy of the Eventgen files used in this book at our download site: https://github.com/PacktPublishing/Splunk-7-Essentials-Third-Edition.
2. Extract the ZIP file to the root location for your environment.
3. Rename the extracted folder to SA-Eventgen. In Windows, this can be done with the Windows GUI, or via the mv command in Linux.
4. Open an administrator Command Prompt or Linux shell and execute the following command (the slashes are important):

    ```
    Windows: C:> xcopy SA-Eventgen C:\Splunk\etc\apps\SA-Eventgen /O /X
    /E /H /K
    Linux: mv SA-Eventgen /$SPLUNK_HOME/etc/apps/
    ```

5. In the prompt, type the following directory command to verify that the copy works properly and the contents are in the folder:

    ```
    Windows: C:> dir C:\Splunk\etc\apps\SA-Eventgen
    Linux: ls -l /$SPLUNK_HOME/etc/apps/
    ```

These are the contents of the recently copied SA-Eventgen folder, as shown in the following (Windows) screenshot, the same as what would appear in the similar location on Linux:

```
C:\>dir C:\Splunk\etc\apps\SA-Eventgen
 Volume in drive C is OS
 Volume Serial Number is F0A3-9A9B

 Directory of C:\Splunk\etc\apps\SA-Eventgen

01/09/2018  09:40 AM    <DIR>          .
01/09/2018  09:40 AM    <DIR>          ..
01/09/2018  09:34 AM               176 .gitignore
01/09/2018  09:34 AM               128 artifacts.conf
01/09/2018  09:40 AM    <DIR>          bin
01/09/2018  09:34 AM               651 build.sh
01/09/2018  09:34 AM             1,968 build.xml
01/09/2018  09:40 AM    <DIR>          default
01/09/2018  09:40 AM    <DIR>          lib
01/09/2018  09:34 AM            11,358 LICENSE
01/09/2018  09:40 AM    <DIR>          metadata
01/09/2018  09:40 AM    <DIR>          README
01/09/2018  09:34 AM            11,802 README.md
01/09/2018  09:40 AM    <DIR>          samples
01/09/2018  09:40 AM    <DIR>          tests
               6 File(s)         26,083 bytes
               9 Dir(s)  875,449,962,496 bytes free
```

6. Return to the Splunk interface in your web browser and restart Splunk by selecting the **Settings** dropdown; under the **SYSTEM** section, click on **Server controls**:

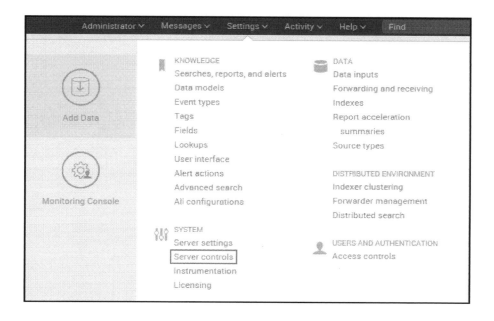

7. On the **Server controls** page, click on the **Restart Splunk** button. Click on **OK** when asked to confirm the restart.

8. The web interface will first notify you that Splunk is restarting in the background, then it will tell you that the restart has been successful. Every time Splunk is restarted, you will be prompted to log in with your credentials. Go ahead and log in.

9. After logging in, you will now see the Eventgen app in the Splunk Enterprise landing page. Go to the **Manage Apps** page and confirm that the **SA-EventGen** application is installed:

You have successfully installed a Splunk add-on.

Controlling Splunk

There are several different ways to stop, start, or restart Splunk. The easiest way to restart Splunk is to do it from the web interface, as demonstrated in the preceding section. The web interface, however, only allows you to restart your Splunk instance. It does not offer any other control options.

The most flexible way to control Splunk is by using the CLI. Using the CLI is an essential skill for Splunk administrators.

In the console or Command Prompt, type in the following command and hit *Enter* on your keyboard:

```
Windows: C:\> cd C:\Splunk\bin
Linux: cd /$SPLUNK_HOME/bin
```

While in the $SPLUNK_HOME/bin directory, issue the following command to restart Splunk:

```
Windows: C:\Splunk\bin>splunk restart
Linux: [user@server bin]$ ./splunk restart
```

After issuing this command, splunkd will go through its restart process. Here are the other basic parameters that you can pass to the Splunk application to control Splunk:

Windows:

- splunk status: Tells you whether splunkd is running or not
- splunk stop: Stops splunkd and all its processes
- splunk start: Starts splunkd and all its processes
- splunk restart: Restarts splunkd and all its processes

Linux:

- ./splunk status: Tells you whether splunkd is running or not
- ./splunk stop: Stops splunkd and all its processes
- ./splunk start: Starts splunkd and all its processes
- ./splunk restart: Restarts splunkd and all its processes

Doing this from a CLI gives the added benefit of verbose messages. A verbose message is a message with a lot of information in it. Such messages can be useful for making sure the system is working correctly or troubleshooting any errors.

A successful **restart** of `splunkd` generally has the following output (elements of which may vary):

```
C:\Splunk\bin>splunk restart
Splunkd: Stopped

Splunk> 4TW

Checking prerequisites...
        Checking http port [8000]: open
        Checking mgmt port [8089]: open
        Checking appserver port [127.0.0.1:8065]: open
        Checking kvstore port [8191]: open
        Checking configuration...  Done.
        Checking critical directories...        Done
        Checking indexes...
                Validated: _audit _internal _introspection _telemetry _thefishbucket history main summary
        Done
        Checking filesystem compatibility...  Done
        Checking conf files for problems...
        Done
        Checking default conf files for edits...
        Validating installed files against hashes from 'C:\Splunk\splunk-7.0.1-2b5b15c4ee89-windows-64-manifest'
        All installed files intact.
        Done
All preliminary checks passed.

Starting splunk server daemon (splunkd)...

Splunkd: Starting (pid 12720)
Done


Waiting for web server at http://127.0.0.1:8000 to be available. Done


If you get stuck, we're here to help.
Look for answers here: http://docs.splunk.com

The Splunk web interface is at http://DESKTOP-M9BQ20N:8000

C:\Splunk\bin>
```

In Windows, you can also control Splunk through the **Splunkd Service**, as shown in the following screenshot. The **d** in the service name, denoting daemon, means a background process. Note that the second service, **splunkweb**, is not running. Do not try to start **splunkweb** as it is deprecated and is there only for legacy purposes. The Splunk-running web application is now bundled in **Splunkd Service**:

Software Protection	Enables the ...		Automatic (D...	Network S...
Splunkd Service	Splunkd is t...	Running	Automatic	Local Syste...
splunkweb (legacy purposes only)	The splunk...		Automatic	Local Syste...
Spot Verifier	Verifies pote...		Manual (Trig...	Local Syste...

Configuring Eventgen

We are almost there. Proceed by first downloading the exercise materials that will be used in this book. Open an administrator Command Prompt and make sure you are in the root of the Windows machine or Linux user shell. Download the ZIP file and extract it in your computer using `https://github.com/PacktPublishing/Splunk-7-Essentials-Third-Edition`.

The Eventgen configuration you will need for the exercises in this book has been packaged and is ready to go. We are not going into the details of how to configure Eventgen. If you are interested in learning more about Eventgen, visit the project page at `http://github.com/splunk/eventgen`.

Follow these instructions to proceed:

1. Extract the project ZIP file into your local machine. Open an administrator console and use the change directory command to set where you extracted the file.

2. Create a new `samples` directory in the **Destinations** Splunk app. The path of this new directory will be `$SPLUNK_HOME/etc/apps/destinations/samples`:

```
Windows: C:> mkdir C:\Splunk\etc\apps\destinations\samples
Linux: mkdir /splunk/etc/apps/destinations/samples
```

3. Copy all the `*.sample` files from `/labs/chapter01/eventgen` of the extracted project directory into the newly created `samples` directory. Windows users can also copy and paste using a GUI:

```
Windows: C:> copy C:\splunk-essentials-
            master\labs\chapter01\eventgen\*.sample
         C:\Splunk\etc\apps\destinations\samples
Linux: cp /splunk-essentials-
       master/labs/chapter01/eventgen/*.sample
/splunk/etc/apps/destinations/samples
```

4. Now, copy the `eventgen.conf` into the `$SPLUNK_HOME/etc/apps/destinations/local` directory. Windows users can also copy and paste using the GUI if you prefer:

```
Windows: C:> copy C:\splunk-essentials-master\labs
         \chapter01\eventgen\eventgen.conf
           C:\Splunk\etc\apps\destinations\local
Linux:   cp /splunk-essentials-master/labs/chapter01/eventgen.conf
         /splunk/etc/apps/destinations/local
```

5. Grant the `SYSTEM` Windows account full access permissions to the `eventgen.conf` file. This is a very important step. You can either do it using the following `icacls` command or change it using the Windows GUI. This step (*Step 5*) is not required for Linux users, who can move on to *Step 6*:

```
C:> icacls C:\Splunk\etc\apps\destinations\local\eventgen.conf
           /grant SYSTEM:F
```

A successful output of this command will look like this:

```
processed file: C:\Splunk\etc\apps\destinations\local\eventgen.conf
        Successfully processed 1 files; Failed processing 0 files
```

6. Restart Splunk.

Viewing the Destinations app

Next we will see our **Destinations** app in action! Remember that we have configured it to draw events from a prototype web company. That is what we did when we set it up to work with Eventgen. Now, let's look at some of our data:

1. After a successful restart, log back in to Splunk and proceed to your new **Destinations** app:

2. In the **Search** field, type this search query and select *Enter*:

```
SPL> index=main
```

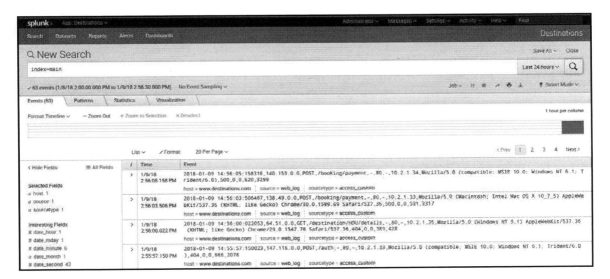

Examine the event data that your new app is enabling to come into Splunk. You will see a lot of references to browsers, systems, and so forth, the kinds of information that make a web-based e-commerce company run.

Try changing the time range to **Real-time (5 minute window)** to see the data flow in before your eyes:

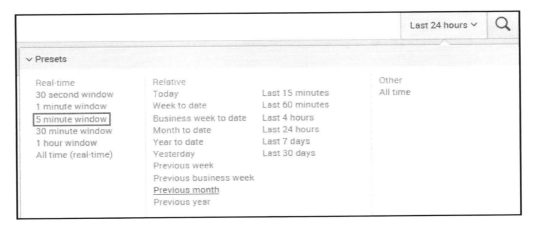

Congratulations! You now have real-time web log data that we can use in subsequent chapters.

Tip from the Fez: Running a Splunk report under a real-time window places heavier strain on Splunk because it is rerunning the search over and over to generate the live nature of the real-time window. Unless absolutely needed, choose to have reports run for a set time period on user demand or a previously assigned schedule.

Creating your first dashboard

Now that we have data in Splunk, it's time to use it in order to derive something meaningful out of it. You are still in the **Destinations** app, correct? We will show you the basic routine when creating new dashboards and dashboard panels.

Type in or copy/paste the following search query in the **Search Field**, then hit *Enter*:

```
SPL> index=main /booking/confirmation earliest=-24h@h | timechart
     count span=15m
```

After the search results render, click on the **Visualization** tab. This will switch your view into a visualization so you can readily see how your data will look. By default, it should already be using the **Column Chart** as shown in the following screenshot. If it does not, then use the screenshot as a guide on how to set it:

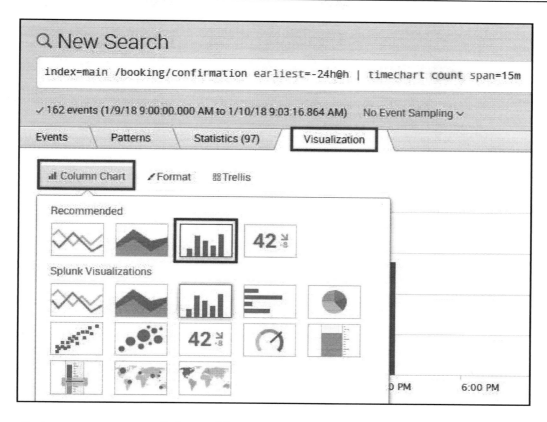

Now that you can see your **Column Chart**, it is time to save it as a dashboard. Click on **Save As** in the upper-right corner of the page, then select **Dashboard Panel**, as shown in the following screenshot:

Now, let's fill up that dashboard panel information, as seen in the following screenshot. Make sure to select the **Shared in App** in the **Dashboard Permissions** section:

Finish up by clicking **View Dashboard** in the next prompt:

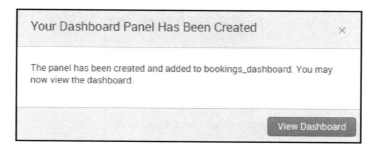

You have created your very first Splunk dashboard with a single panel telling you the number of confirmed bookings in the last 24 hours at 15-minute intervals. If you let Eventgen run for a while and rerun the dashboard, the contents will populate as the data is generated. Time to show it to your boss!

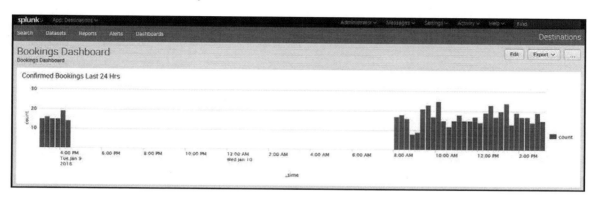

In one chapter we acquired, installed, and used Splunk. We now have a fully-functional Splunk installation with live data. Leave Splunk running for two hours or so. After a few hours, you can stop Splunk if you need to rest for a bit to suppress indexing and restart it when you're ready to proceed into the next chapters.

Do you recall how to control Splunk from the command line?

```
Windows:      C:\Splunk\bin> splunk stop
              C:\Splunk\bin> splunk start
              C:\Splunk\bin> splunk restart
Linux:        bin]$ ./splunk stop
              bin]$ ./splunk start
              bin]$ ./splunk restart
```

Summary

In this chapter, you learned a number of basic Splunk concepts that you need to get started with this powerful tool. You learned how to install Splunk and configure a new Splunk app. You ran a simple search against the Splunk internal logs to ensure that the application is functional. You then installed a Splunk add-on called **Eventgen**, which you used to populate dummy data into Splunk in real time. You were shown how to control Splunk using the web user interface and the CLI. Finally, you created your very first Splunk dashboard, based off a single search. We will get a lot more creative with dashboards in additional chapters later in this book.

Now, we will go on to Chapter 2, *Bringing in Data*, to learn more about how to input data.

Bringing in Data

2

Computerized systems are responsible for much of the data produced on a daily basis. Splunk Enterprise makes it easy to get data from many of these systems. This data is frequently referred to as machine data. And since machines mostly generate data in an ongoing or streaming nature, Splunk is especially useful as it can handle streaming data easily and efficiently.

In addition to capturing machine data, Splunk Enterprise allows you, as the user, to enhance and enrich the data either as it is stored or as it is searched. Machine data can be enriched with business rules and logic for enhanced searching capabilities. Often it is combined with traditional row/column data to provide business context to machine data with data such a product hierarchies.

In this chapter, you will learn about Splunk and how it relates to a often used term - big data, as well as the most common methods of ingesting data into Splunk. The chapter will also introduce essential concepts such as forwarders, indexes, events, event types, fields, sources, and sourcetypes. It is paramount that you learn this early on as it will empower you to get the most value from your data. In this chapter, we will cover the following topics:

- Splunk and big data
- Splunk data sources
- Splunk indexes
- Inputting data into Splunk
- Splunk events and fields

Splunk and big data

Big data is a widely used term but, as is often the case, one that means different things to different people. In this part of the chapter, we present common characteristics of big data .

There is no doubt that today there is a lot of data, and more commonly today, the term big data is not meant to reference the volume as much as it is characterized by other factors, including variability so wide that legacy, conventional organizational data systems cannot consume and produce analytics from it.

Streaming data

Streaming data is almost always being generated, with a timestamp associated to each entry. Splunk's inherent ability to monitor and track data loaded from ever growing log files, or accept data as it arrives on a port, are critical pieces of functionality.

However, streaming data is no different than other data in that it's usefulness erodes, particularly at a detailed level. For instance, consider a firewall log.

In real time, Splunk will capture and index events written to a firewall log file. Normally, there will be many different activity events logged to Splunk in real time. However, many of those events are normal logging events noting activity occurring successfully.

As you consider your source data, its important to consider how long you want to retain data and/or how you would want to archive it. It is also important to understand if you need all the data from the source or only specific kinds of events.

Analytical data latency

The term latency, in regards to data, refers to the time it takes from data being captured to it being available for reporting any analysis.

Splunk is able to capture and analyze data in real time (that is, in under one second, often in hundredths or tenths of a second) when deployed on appropriately sized hardware. For example, if a Splunk alert triggers, it can run a script to immediately execute a server shut down. If a denial-of-service attack (a cyber attack that can dramatically hurt an e-commerce company's bottom line) is taking place, Splunk can be used to figure out what is happening in real time.

If data is not available in real time, Splunk can monitor and capture when the data is made available, run data capture services on a scheduled basis pending the nature of the source data and system, or just listen on a server port awaiting for and accepting data once it arrives.

Sparseness of data

Splunk is also excellent for dealing with sparse data. Much data in retailing environments is considered sparse. Consider a store that has many products but where most people just buy a few of them on any given shopping trip. If the store's database has fields specifying how many items of a particular type have been purchased by each customer, most of the fields would be empty if the time interval under consideration was short. We would say then that the data is sparse. In Splunk, the sparseness of data in a search ranges from dense (meaning that a result is obtained 10 percent of the time or more) to sparse (from 0.01 to 1 percent of the time). This can also extend to super sparse, or for a better definition, trying to find a needle in a haystack (which is less than 0.01 percent), and even to rare, which is just a handful of cases.

Splunk data sources

Splunk was invented as a way to keep track of and analyze machine data coming from a variety of computerized systems. It is a powerful platform for doing just that. But since its invention, it has been used for a myriad of different data types, including streaming log data, database and spreadsheet data, and data provided by web services. The various types of data that Splunk is often used for are explained in the next few sections.

Machine data

As mentioned previously, much of Splunk's data capability is focused on machine data. Machine data is data created each time a machine does something, even if it is as seemingly insignificant as a successful user login. Each event has information about its exact time (down to the second or millisecond) and source, and each of these becomes a field associated with the event. The term **machine data** can be used in reference to a wide variety of data coming from computerized machines, from servers to operating systems to controllers for robotic assembly arms. Almost all machine data includes the time it was created or when the actual event took place. If no timestamp is included, then Splunk will need to find a date in the source name or filename based on the file's last modification time. As a last resort, it will stamp the event with the time it was indexed into Splunk.

Web logs

Web logs are invaluable sources of information for anyone interested in learning about how their website is used. Deep analysis of web logs can answer questions about which pages are visited the most, which pages have problems (people leaving quickly, discarded shopping carts, coding errors, and other aborted actions), and many others.

Data files

Splunk can read data from basically all types of files. Splunk can also decompress the following types of files: `tar`, `gz`, `bz2`, `tar.gz`, `tgz`, `tbz`, `tbz2`, `zip`, and `z`, along with many others.

Social media data

An enormous amount of data is produced by social media every second. Consider the fact that 1.37 billion people (`https://zephoria.com/top-15-valuable-facebook-statistics/`) log in to Facebook each day, and they spend on an average 20 minutes at a time interacting with the site. Any Facebook (or any other social media) interaction creates a significant amount of data, even if it doesn't include the more data-intensive acts, such as posting a picture, audio file, or a video. Other social media sources of data include popular sites such as Twitter, Instagram, and LinkedIn in the United States and QZone, WeChat, and Weibo in China. As a result of the increasing number of social media sites, the volume of social media data and machine data generated by the information technology infrastructure running these sites continues to grow dramatically each year.

Relational database data

Splunk provides a free app called **DB Connect**, and, with it, you can easily and quickly connect to relational database management systems such as Oracle and Microsoft SQL Server. DB Connect provides three major functionalities as it relates to relational database data:

- Import data from database tables into Splunk with a SQL Query
- Export data from Splunk into database tables mapping Splunk fields to database table fields

- Execute runtime look-ups to gather reference data, such as a customer or product hierarchy often stored in databases, to provide organizational context to event data

Other data types

Almost any type of data works in Splunk. Some of these types include scripted inputs and modular inputs. Sometimes you may want to include a script that sets data up so that it is indexed the way you want. Or you may want to include data coming from a source that is unusual in some way, and you want to make sure that the fields are set up the way they should be. For these reasons, it is nice to know that you can use Python scripts, Windows batch files, shell scripts, and other utilities to make sure your inputs are formatted correctly. You will see the other data types listed when we add data to Splunk shortly.

Creating indexes

Indexes are where Splunk Enterprise stores all the data it has processed. It is essentially a collection of databases that are, by default, located at `$SPLUNK_HOME/var/lib/splunk`. Before data can be searched, it needs to be indexed—a process we describe here.

Tip from the Fez: There are a variety of intricate settings which can be manipulated to control size and data management aspects of an index. We will not cover those in this book, however as your situation requires complexity, be sure to consider a variety of topics around index management, such as overall size, buckets parameters, archiving and other optimization settings.

There are two ways to create an index, through the Splunk user interface or by creating an `indexes.conf` file. You will be shown here how to create an index using the Splunk portal, but you should realize that when you do that, it simply generates an `indexes.conf` file.

When adding and making changes to configurations in the Splunk user interface, those updates will commonly be stored in a configuration file (`.conf`) somewhere under the `$SPLUNK_HOME` directory.

You will be creating an index called `winlogs` to store a sample Windows `perfmon` log. To do this, take the following steps:

1. In the Splunk navigation bar, go to **Settings**.
2. In the **Data** section, click on **Indexes**, which will take you to the Indexes page.
3. Click on the **New Index** button in the upper-right corner.
4. Fill out the information for this new index as seen in the following screenshots, carefully going through *steps 1* to *6*. You will need to scroll down in the window to complete all the steps.

   The following screenshot displays the first three steps to be followed:

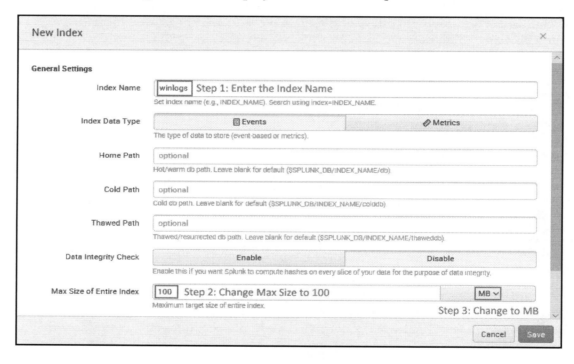

The next screenshot indicates step 4 and step 5 to be followed:

New Index ×

Data Integrity Check	Enable	Disable

Enable this if you want Splunk to compute hashes on every slice of your data for the purpose of data integrity.

Max Size of Entire Index	100	MB ∨

Maximum target size of entire index.

Max Size of Hot/Warm/Cold Bucket	auto	MB ∨

Maximum target size of buckets. Enter 'auto_high_volume' for high-volume indexes.   **Step 4: Change to MB**

Frozen Path	optional

Frozen bucket archive path. Set this if you want Splunk to automatically archive frozen buckets.

App	Destinations ∨

Storage Optimization   Step 5: Change to the Destinations App

Tsidx Retention Policy	Enable Reduction	Disable Reduction

Warning: Do not enable reduction without understanding the full implications. It is extremely difficult to rebuild reduced buckets. Learn More ☑

Reduce tsidx files older than		Days ∨

Age is determined by the latest event in a bucket.

Step 6: Hit Save

Cancel   Save

5. Be sure to **Save** when you are done.

You will now see the new index in the list as shown here:

winlogs	Edit Delete Disable	🗐 Events	destinations	1 MB	100 MB

The preceding steps have created a new `indexes.conf` file.

Now go ahead and inspect this file. In Windows this can be done through Notepad. In Linux, you can use a visual text editor such as Notepad++ to connect to your Linux server or, at the command line, use `vi`.

The specific `indexes.conf` to open will be found in `$SPLUNK_HOME\etc\apps\destinations\local`. Specifying the destinations app for the index is what placed the `indexes.conf` file below the destinations directory.

Tip from the Fez: As you build your Splunk environment, organize your content by application. This will ensure that the configurations can be stored and managed consistently as needed, as opposed to storing all configurations inside a single application. The challenges with this approach will become more evident as your Splunk environment grows.

Every index has specific settings of its own. Here is how your index looks when automatically configured by the portal. In production environments, this is how Splunk administrators manage indexes:

```
[winlogs]
coldPath = $SPLUNK_DB\winlogs\colddb
enableDataIntegrityControl = 0
enableTsidxReduction = 0
homePath = $SPLUNK_DB\winlogs\db
maxTotalDataSizeMB = 100
thawedPath = $SPLUNK_DB\winlogs\thaweddb
```

Note that the maximum size value of 100 that you specified is also indicated in the configuration.

The complete `indexes.conf` documentation can be found at `http://docs.splunk.com/Documentation/Splunk/latest/admin/indexesconf`.

Buckets

You may have noticed that there is a certain pattern in this configuration file, in which folders are broken into three locations: `coldPath`, `homePath`, and `thawedPath`. This is a very important concept in Splunk. An index contains compressed raw data and associated index files which are spread out into age-designated directories. Each age-designated directory is called a **bucket**.

A bucket moves through several stages as it ages. In general, as your data gets older (think colder) in the system, it is pushed to the next bucket. And, as you can see in the following list, the thawed bucket contains data that has been restored from an archive. Here is a breakdown of the buckets in relation to each other:

- **hot**: This is newly indexed data and open for writing (`hotPath`)
- **warm**: This is data rolled from the hot bucket with no active writing (`warmPath`)

- **cold**: This is data rolled from the warm bucket (`coldPath`)
- **frozen**: This is data rolled from the cold bucket and archived (`frozenPath`)
- **thawed**: This is data restored from the archive (`thawedPath`)

Tip from the Fez: By default, Splunk will delete data as opposed to archiving it in a frozen bucket. Ensure that you are aware of the data retention requirements for your application and configure a path for frozen buckets to land if required.

Now going back to the `indexes.conf` file, you should realize that `homePath` will contain the hot and warm buckets, `coldPath` will contain the cold bucket, and `thawedPath` will contain any restored data from the archive. This means you can put buckets in different locations to efficiently manage storage resources.

For our purposes, we have chosen to let Splunk handle when data rolls from one bucket to the next using default settings. In high-volume environments, you may need to more specifically control when data rolls through bucket process.

Log files as data input

As mentioned earlier in this chapter, any configuration you make in the Splunk portal corresponds to a `*.conf` file written under the `$SPLUNK_HOME` directory. The same goes for the creation of data inputs; adding data inputs using the Splunk user interface creates a file called `inputs.conf`.

For this exercise use the `windows_perfmon_logs.txt` file provided in the `Chapter 2/samples`.

Now that you have an index to store Windows logs, let's create a data input for it, with the following steps:

1. Go to the Splunk home page.
2. Click on your **Destinations** app. Make sure you are in the **Destinations** app before you execute the next steps, or your configuration changes won't be isolated to your application.
3. In the Splunk navigation bar, select **Settings**.

4. Under the **Data** section, click on **Data inputs**.
5. On the **Data inputs** page, click on **Files & directories**.
6. In the next page, click on the **New** button.
7. Locate the `windows_perfmon_logs.txt` file from the `Chapter 2/samples` and select it.
8. Ensure **Continuously Monitor** is selected. Your selections should resemble the following screenshot:

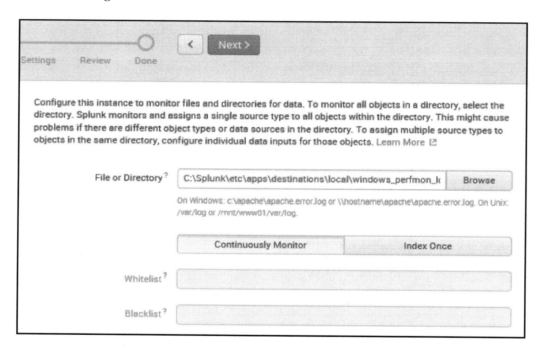

9. However, if you're using a Linux machine, your selections should resemble the following screenshot:

Configure this instance to monitor files and directories for data. To monitor all objects in a directory, select the directory. Splunk monitors and assigns a single source type to all objects within the directory. This might cause problems if there are different object types or data sources in the directory. To assign multiple source types to objects in the same directory, configure individual data inputs for those objects. Learn More ⧉

File or Directory ? `C:\Splunk\etc\apps\destinations\local\windows_perfmon_l` **Browse**

On Windows: c:\apache\apache.error.log or \\hostname\apache\apache.error.log. On Unix: /var/log or /mnt/www01/var/log.

Continuously Monitor   **Index Once**

Whitelist ?

Blacklist ?

10. Click on **Next** to advance to the set source type screen. While not defaulting to a specific value, Splunk recognizes the files characters and applies proper line breaking for the source file in question.

11. Click on **Save As** to enter the custom sourcetype as **myperfmon**. Ensure the category for the sourcetype is **Custom** and the app is your **Destinations** app. Finally, click on the **Save** button to save your new custom sourcetype.

12. Click on the **Next** button at the top of the screen to proceed to the next step in the data input process.

13. In the input setting window, ensure that the app context is **Destinations (destinations)** and set the index for this data input to the `winlogs` index we created earlier in this chapter.

14. Click on the **Review** button to proceed to the final review step.

15. Click on **Submit** to complete the data input setup process.

16. Click on the **Start Searching** button on the following screen to ensure the data from the `perfmon` sample file is being loaded. As in the Windows example screenshot shown as follows, the source and the sourcetype associated with the raw events are called out as **Selected Fields**:

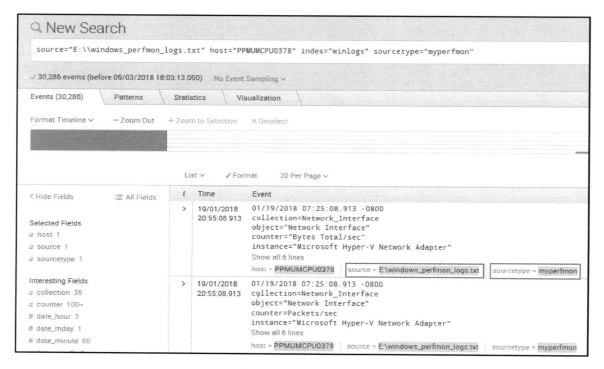

We have introduced a new concept here called **sourcetype**. A sourcetype is a type of classification of data that has been automatically made for you when you created the data input through the Splunk portal. There will be more about sourcetypes in `Chapter 3`, *Search Processing Language*. In our preceding example, classifying the data input as `myperfmon` would allow us to easily search as well as provide specific rules to this data, as opposed to other windows log data we may want to store in the same index.

Go ahead and inspect the `inputs.conf` file:

1. View the following file:

    `$SPLUNK_HOME/etc/apps/destinations/local/inputs.conf`

2. Compare your results with this `inputs.conf` entry and ensure that it is the same (Windows first, and then Linux):

```
Windows: [monitor://C:Splunk\windows_perfmon_logs.txt]
         disabled = false
         index = winlogs
         sourcetype = myperfmon
  Linux: [monitor:///home/jp/windows_perfmon_logs.txt]
         disabled = fales
         index = winlogs
         sourcetype = myperfmon
```

Seasoned Splunk administrators may add data inputs directly to the `inputs.conf` file instead of using the user interface, and may require a Splunk restart.

The complete documentation for the `inputs.conf` file can be found at `https://docs.splunk.com/Documentation/Splunk/latest/Admin/Inputsconf`.

If you closely followed the instructions in this book, you should now have the data sources you need in your very own Splunk system used in the remainder of the book.

Splunk events and fields

All throughout this chapter, you have been running Splunk search queries that have returned data. It is important to understand what events and fields are before we go any further, for an understanding of these is essential to comprehending what happens when you run Splunk on the data.

In Splunk, data is classified into events and is like a record, such as a log file entry or other type of input data. An event can have many different attributes or fields or just a few. When you run a successful search query, you will see events returned from the Splunk indexes the search is being run against. If you are looking at live streaming data, events can come in very quickly through Splunk.

Every event is given a number of default fields. For a complete listing, go to `http://docs.splunk.com/Documentation/Splunk/6.3.2/Data/Aboutdefaultfields`. We will now go through some of these default fields:

- **Timestamp**: A timestamp is applied as the event is indexed in Splunk. Splunk typically determines what timestamp to assign from the raw data it receives. For example, as a shopper clicks on the final purchase button on an e-commerce website, data is collected about precisely when the sale occurred. Splunk can usually automatically detect this from the raw data.
- **Host**: The host field tells us what the hostname, IP address, or full domain name of the data is.
- **Index**: The index field describes where the event is stored, giving the specific name of the index.
- **Source**: The source field tells us where the data came from, specifically the file, data stream, or other data input.
- **Sourcetype**: The sourcetype is the format of the data input from which the data came. Common sourcetypes are `access_combined`, `access_custom`, and `cisco_syslog`.
- **Linecount**: The linecount is simply the number of lines contained in the event.

These default fields are key/value pairings that are added to events when Splunk indexes data. Think of fields as a quick way to categorize and group events. Fields are the primary constituents of all search queries. In later chapters, you will learn more about fields and how to create custom fields from events.

Extracting new fields

Most raw data that you will encounter will have some form of structure. Just like a **CSV** (**comma-separated value**) file or a web log file, it is assumed that each entry in the log corresponds to some sort of format. Splunk makes custom field extraction very easy, especially for delimited files. Let's take the case of our Eventgen data and look at the following example. By design, the raw data generated by Eventgen is delimited by commas. Following is a example of a raw event:

```
2018-01-18 21:19:20:013632, 130.253.37.97,GET,/destination/PML/details,-
,80,- 10.2.1.33,Mozilla/5.0 (iPad; U; CPU OS 4_3_3 like Mac OS X; en-us)
AppleWebKit/533.17.9 (KHTML, like Gecko) Version/5.0.2 Mobile/8J3
Safari/6533.18.5,301,0,0,317,1514
```

Since there is a distinct separation of fields in this data, we can use Splunk's field extraction capabilities to automatically classify values of data into fields, which can then be used for easy searching and filtering:

1. In your **Destinations** app Search page, run the following search command:

   ```
   SPL> index=main sourcetype=access_custom
   ```

   The sourcetype `access_custom` refers to a type of file format that is generated by a server as it creates a web log file. After the data populates from running the preceding search, click on the **Extract New Fields** link in the left column of the page, as shown in this screenshot:

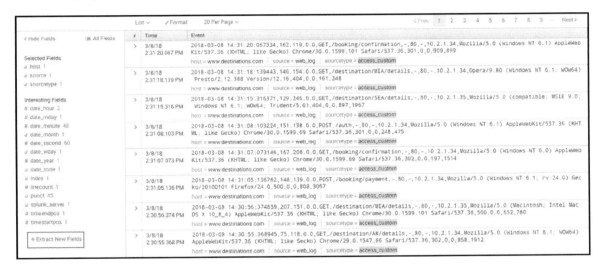

The highlighted text indicates Extract New Fields

2. In the resulting **Extract Fields** page, select one of the events that is shown in the
   `_raw` events area. Try to select the entry with the longest text. As soon as you do
   this, the text will appear highlighted at the top of the page, as per the following
   screenshot:

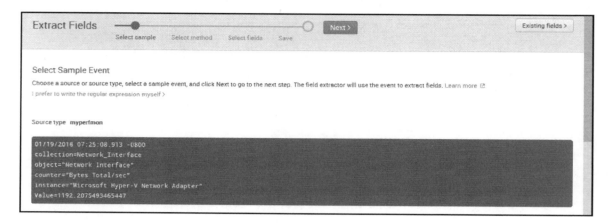

3. Click on the **Next** button to proceed. In the page that appears, click on the
   Delimiters icon, which will turn blue after clicking on it, as indicated in the
   following screenshot:

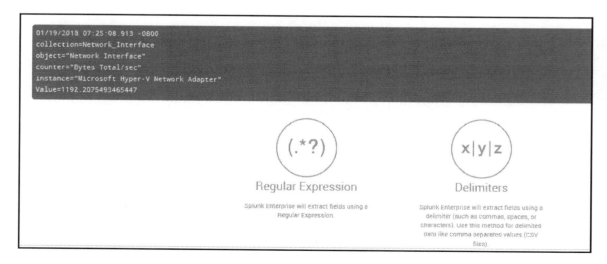

4. Click on **Next**. On the next page, click on the **Comma** delimiter as shown in this screenshot:

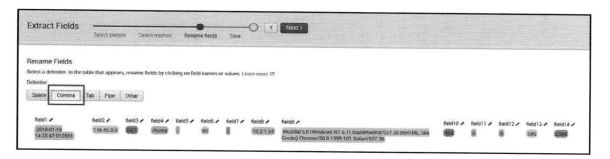

As soon as you select the **Comma** delimiter, Splunk will automatically allow you to modify each field and add a label to it.

5. Click on the pencil icon for each field to input the label. When you're done, click on the **Rename Field** icon.

Provide names for the remaining fields using the following guide. These fields will be needed in future chapters. You can skip those that are not included in the following list:

- **field1**: `datetime`
- **field2**: `client_ip`
- **field3**: `http_method`
- **field4**: `http_uri`
- **field8**: `server_ip`
- **field9**: `http_user_agent`
- **field10**: `http_status_code`
- **field14**: `http_response_time`

When you have completed the preceding task, click on **Next** to proceed. In the next window, label the **Extractions Name** as **eventgen** and select the **All apps** permission type. Refer to the following screenshot:

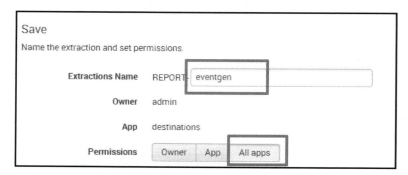

6. Click on **Finish** to complete the process. Now that you have extracted new fields, these will be readily available in your search queries.

7. In the resulting screen, click on **Explore the fields I just created in Search**:

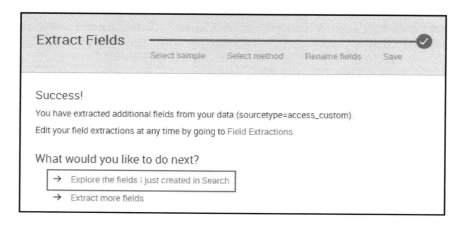

When the events appear, the field names you just entered will appear in the fields list:

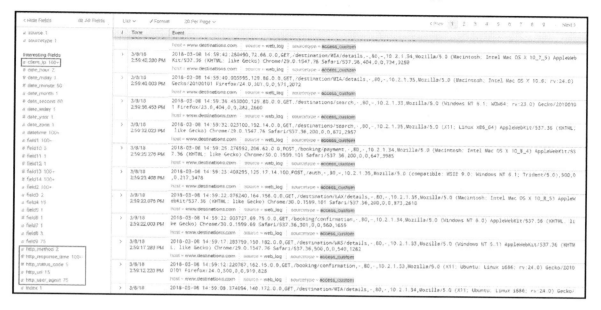

Highlighted text indicating field names added

As mentioned earlier, additional configurations added to Splunk after installation are contained in `.conf` files. Check out these files to see where the configurations you just created now live at the filesystem level:

$SPLUNK_HOME/etc/apps/destinations/local/props.conf

$SPLUNK_HOME/etc/apps/destinations/local/transforms.conf

When using custom datasets and/or advanced configurations for parsing data, the entries will reside in these files, which all work together from sourcing data to loading it and reporting on it properly. There is a significant amount of online document related to these files.

Tip from the Fez: When creating custom sourcetypes, often Splunk will not conveniently recognize the file contents, like our previous example. The following configurations can be modified via the Splunk user interface and are stored in `props.conf`, where they can also be modified. These configurations should be reviewed and implemented where necessary to ensure that your data is loaded accurately:

- `TIME_PREFIX`
- `TIME_FORMAT`
- `LINE_BREAKER`
- `SHOULD_LINEMERGE`
- `MAX_TIMESTAMP_LOOKAHEAD`

Complete documentation for `props.conf` can be found here: `https://docs.splunk.com/Documentation/Splunk/latest/Admin/Propsconf`.

In the next chapter, you will learn how to use these new fields to filter search results.

Summary

In this chapter, we began learning about big data and its related characteristics, such as streaming data, analytical data latency, and sparseness. We also covered the types of data that can be brought into Splunk. We then created an index and loaded a sample log file, all while examining the configuration file (`.conf`) entries made at the file system level. We talked about what fields and events are. And finally, we saw how to extract fields from events and name them so that they can be more useful to us.

In the chapters to come, we'll learn more about these important features of Splunk.

Search Processing Language 3

So far, this book has introduced you to collecting and indexing data with Splunk, which prepares it for searching, and you've seen a few simple search commands too. In this chapter, we will cover more about how to use search and other commands to analyze your data.

In this chapter, we will cover the following topics:

- Anatomy of a search
- Search pipeline
- Time modifiers
- Filtering searches
- Search commands:
  - stats
  - top/rare
  - chart and timechart
  - eval
  - rex

Anatomy of a search

Search processing language (SPL), a special-purpose processing language, was developed to enable fast searching on machine-generated data indexed by Splunk. The language was originally set up to be based on the Unix pipeline and **Standard Query Language** (SQL). SPL (as opposed to SQL) is a library of all search processing commands and their functions, arguments, and clauses. With a search command, you can group different events, filter data based on a constraint, extract fields using regular expressions, perform statistical calculations, and other tasks.

Let's dissect a search query so that you can understand exactly how it works. This will also help you to understand what pipes are. As you will see, a pipe basically takes the data that has come from an earlier step, and after it has been acted on, filtered, or extracted, it sends it on to the next step in processing.

We'll use the **Destinations** app here to show you a simple example:

1. Go to the Splunk home page
2. Click on your **Destinations** app
3. In your **Destinations** app's search page, type in the following:

```
SPL> index=_internal sourcetype=splunk* | top limit=5 name | sort -
name
```

The following diagram will help you visualize the data as it goes through one delimiting pipe (|) to another; in this case, it goes from the internal index of Splunk, to limiting it to the top five names, to sorting by name, which is then sent to the **Final Results** table. We will go through this step by step, as shown in the following screenshot:

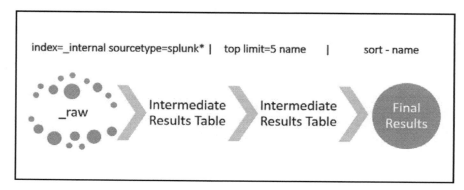

Search pipeline

The arrows in the preceding visualization mean the resulting data from the previous command will be used against the next command in the series. To fully understand this command, let's go through the search pipe by pipe. Type the following commands in succession into the search window, but pause after every one of them and observe how the data changes.

The following command will display the raw events:

```
SPL> index=_internal sourcetype=splunk*
```

The next command uses the raw events gathered from the previous step, keys them on the name field, calculates the number of events for the name field, then limits the results to the top five:

```
SPL> index=_internal sourcetype=splunk* | top limit=5 name
```

Finally, the results table of the | top command is passed (also known as **piped**) on to another command | sort for sorting. Once all activities are complete, the final results are presented in the final output table shown in Splunk:

```
SPL> index=_internal sourcetype=splunk* | top limit=5 name | sort -
    name
```

This chaining of commands is called the **search pipeline**.

Time modifiers

Every time you execute a search, always be aware that you are running a query against a set of data that is bound by date and time. The time-range picker is on the right side of the search bar. Splunk comes with predetermined time modifiers, as seen in the following screenshot. You can also use the time-range picker to set up a custom date/time-range or other advanced ranges (`https://docs.splunk.com/Splexicon:Timerangepicker`):

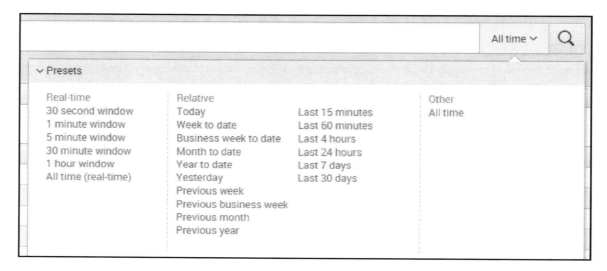

Apart from the **All time** selection, there are two types of time modifiers that will be used the most: **Real-time** and **Relative**. In the preceding screenshot, the predetermined real-time modifiers are in the leftmost column, and the relative time modifiers are in the middle columns.

Real-time modifiers mean that Splunk will run an ongoing, real-time search based on the specified time window. For example, a real-time search that is in a **5 minute window** will continuously display data within the last five minutes. If new data comes in, it will push out the oldest event from the displayed results.

 Tip from the Fez: As we introduced in `Chapter 1`, *Splunk – Getting Started*, real-time searches are resource intensive. Use them sparingly.

Relative time modifiers are just that; they collect data based on relative time, and will find data within the specified time frame. The most common examples as shown earlier in the time-range picker are *to date* (**Week To Date**, **Month To Date**, and so on) and *last X* (**Last 4 hours**, **Last 7 days**, and so on).

What you do not see when you are using the time-range picker is that in the background, Splunk is defining the earliest time and the latest time in specific variables.

The **Last 15 minutes** time-range picker preset, for example, is equivalent to these SPL modifiers:

```
SPL> earliest=-15m latest=now
```

The presets built into Splunk automatically insert the `latest=now` modifier when running its search. Run this search command in your **Destinations** app **Search** bar:

```
SPL> index=main earliest=-8m latest=now | timechart count span=1m
```

Notice that even if you have not changed the time modifier selected in the drop-down menu (which will not change unless you use it), the data will show that your earliest event was 8 minutes ago and your last data is current from point of running the search. In other words, if you put the earliest and latest modifiers in your search, what you manually put in the search overrides the current selection in the time-range picker.

You can use a number of alternative ways to identify each of the time units; the most commonly supported time units listed by Splunk are:

- **Second**: s, sec, secs, second, and seconds
- **Minute**: m, min, minute, minute, and minutes
- **Hour**: h, hr, hrs, hour, and hours
- **Day**: d, day, and days
- **Week**: w, week, and weeks
- **Month**: mon, month, and months
- **Quarter**: q, qtr, qtrs, quarter, and quarters
- **Year**: y, yr, yrs, year, and years

Filtering search results

Splunk is great for searching data. Using search commands, you can filter your results using key phrases just the way you would with a Google search. Here are some examples for you to try out:

```
SPL> index=main /booking/confirmation
```

The preceding filters search results from the index `main`, and only returns those events with the string `/booking/confirmation` in the `_raw` data.

You may also add further filters by adding another phrase. It is very important to note, however, that, by default, Splunk will assume that your phrases are logically chained based on an `AND` operator, for example:

```
SPL> index=main /booking 200
```

The preceding line of code is equivalent to the following:

```
SPL> index=main /booking AND 200
```

Similarly, you can use the `OR` operator to find data based on multiple filters. The following command will return all events with `/booking` or `/destinations` in the text. It is important to remember that an `OR` operator will always give you at least as many (or more) events than an `AND` operator, and `AND` is the default operator:

```
SPL> index=main /booking OR /destinations
```

Like any mathematical operation, you may also use parentheses to group conditions:

```
SPL> index=main (/booking OR /destinations) AND 200
```

If you have a phrase containing a white space, enclose it with quotation marks, as seen in the following example:

```
SPL> index=main "iPhone OS"
```

You may also filter search results using fields. Fields are case-sensitive and a search using a specified field is generally considered faster than a full text search because the filtering is occurring on a known field rather than searching through the entire event to find the value. Filtering using fields will only work if there is a defined field. In Chapter 2, *Bringing in Data*, you extracted new fields from the `eventgen` data source. Let's use that now to filter search results using custom fields:

```
SPL> index=main http_uri=/booking/confirmation AND http_status_code=200
```

Search command – stats

A common use of the `stats` command is to count events. To see how this works, run the following search query. The SPL will return a single number representing the count of all events in the last 30 minutes. Notice that the pipe that precedes the `stats` command filters the data that will be included in the final count:

```
SPL> index=main earliest=-30m latest=now | stats count
```

Change the time modifier and the number should be reduced:

```
SPL> index=main earliest=-15m latest=now | stats count
```

You may be wondering where the count came from. The true format of a `stats` command is `stats function(X)`. This asks the system to return the result of the function based on the field X. When the `count` function is used without parentheses, Splunk assumes that you are looking for the count of all events in the given search.

The `stats` command becomes a very powerful tool especially when you need to group counts by fields. Here is an example:

```
SPL> index=main | stats count by http_method
```

This will result in two rows of data that will show the counts of the GET and the POST methods, as shown in the following screenshot. These are two methods that are used in HTTP (website communication rules for client and server) to ask for information (GET) and submit data (POST):

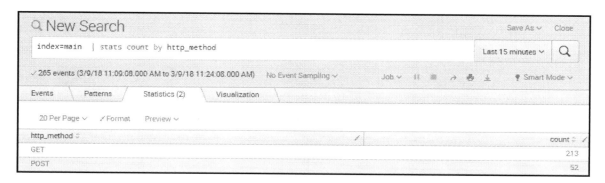

You can also use the `avg(X)` function to get the average value of all the events based on URLs. Here is an example that you can use:

```
SPL> index=main | stats count by http_uri | stats avg(count)
```

Some of the widely used `stats` functions are:

- `avg(X)`: Returns the average of the values of the field `X`
- `dc(X)`: Returns the count of distinct values of the field `X`
- `max(X)`: Returns the maximum value of the field `X`
- `min(X)`: Returns the minimum value of the field `X`
- `perc<X>(Y)`: Returns the Xth percentile of the field `X`, for example `perc95(X)`
- `sum(X)`: Returns the sum of the values of the field `X`

 To learn more about the other `stats` functions, go to `http://docs.splunk.com/Documentation/Splunk/latest/SearchReference/CommonStatsFunctions`.

Search command – top/rare

A quick way to get a summarized table based on the fields is by using the `top` and `rare` commands. Run this search command:

```
SPL> index=main | top http_uri
```

Notice that the result automatically grouped the URLs by count, calculated the percentage of each row against the whole data set, and sorted them by count in descending order. You can see a sample result in the following screenshot:

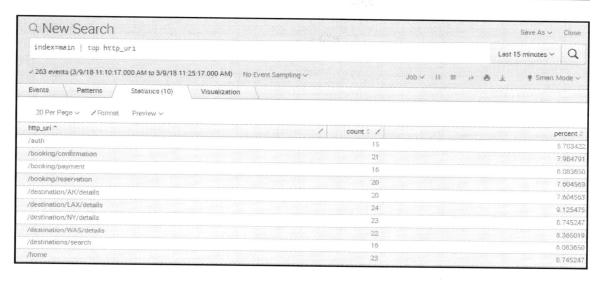

You may further tweak this search command by adding command options such as `limit` and `showperc`. Say, for example, you only want to see the top five URLs, but you do not want to see the percent column. This is the SPL to achieve that:

```
SPL> index=main | top url limit=5 showperc=false
```

Now try the same commands, but use `rare` instead of `top`. The term `rare` will find those events that are the most unlikely ones. This can be a useful qualifier to use for determining outliers or unusual cases that may be due to data entry errors.

Search commands – chart and timechart

The `chart` command aggregates data, providing output in tabular format which can then be used for a visualization. Visualizing data is critical to end user analysis, which makes chart a very important command. Notice that if you run the following search query, it is identical to the output of the `stats` command:

```
SPL> index=main | chart count by http_method
```

For all basic purposes, you can use `stats` and `chart` interchangeably. However, there will be differences in how `stats` and `chart` group data together. It will be up to you to determine which one is your intended result. To show the differences, here are some examples:

```
SPL> index=main | stats count by http_method http_uri
```

You can see the result in the following screenshot:

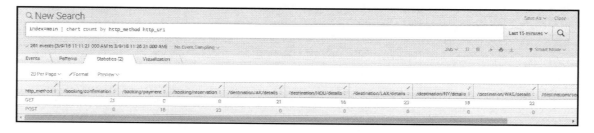

Following is another example:

```
SPL> index=main | chart count by http_method http_uri
```

You can see the result in the following screenshot:

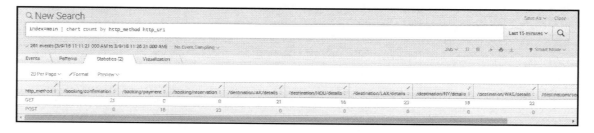

Using the `stats` command, the data was presented as a list where all values were in a single column. The `chart` command, however, places values in cells defined by a row/column location. This is the way to setup the output for graphing based on X/Y types of coordination where there are multiple axes on visualizations such as bar and line charts.

The `timechart` command, on the other hand, creates a time series output with statistical aggregation of the indicated fields. This command is widely used when creating different types of charts where one access of the visualization is time. The most common use of `timechart` is for examining the trends of metrics over time for visualizations including line charts, column charts, bar charts, and area charts, among others:

```
SPL> index=main earliest=-4h latest=now | timechart span=15m count by
http_uri
```

An important option that is part of the `timechart` command is span. The span essentially determines how it will group the data based on time. `span=15m` means it will aggregate the data into 15 minute increments.

The statistical result of the command looks like this:

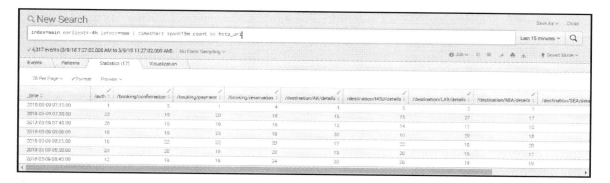

Although admittedly the preceding data looks dull, this very information, when viewed in the **Visualizations** tab, looks much more interesting, as seen in the following screenshot. There will be more on creating dashboard panels and dashboards in `Chapter 6`, *Panes of Glass*:

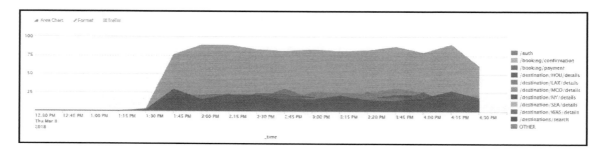

Tip From the Fez: When presenting visualizations using the `timechart` command, Splunk will limit the number of distinct output values to the default of 10, and group remaining results into an 11th data element of **OTHER**. Adding `limit=0` after the `timechart` command will force Splunk to present all distinct output values.

Search command – eval

The `eval` command is perhaps the most advanced and powerful command in SPL. It allows you to store the resulting value of the `eval` operation in a field. A myriad of functions can be used with `eval`. Let us try some of the simpler and more common ones.

The simplest type of `eval` command performs a simple `if/then/else` condition and stores a value in the newly created field. For example, if you want to create counts of successful and unsuccessful requests, use `http_status_code` to determine whether the request is successful, and, if it is, count the transaction as successful:

```
SPL> index=main earliest=-1h latest=now | stats
count(eval(if(http_status_code < "400", 1, NULL))) AS successful_requests
count(eval(if(http_status_code >= "400", 1, NULL))) AS
unsuccessful_requests by http_status_code
```

There are also countless functions that can be used effectively with `eval` (we'll discuss some of them later):

```
SPL> | eval round(X, Y)
```

Run the `search` command shown as follows, then modify it to include the `eval` function `round(X, Y)`. Watch how the percent column values are transformed as they are rounded to the nearest integer with two decimal values:

```
SPL> index=main | top http_uri

index=main | top http_uri | eval percent=round(percent, 2)
```

Use this function to transform the URL strings into uppercase:

```
SPL> index=main | top http_uri

index=main | top http_uri | eval http_uri=upper(http_uri)
```

The `case` function is especially useful when transforming data based on a Boolean condition. If X is true, then assign to the variable the string Y. Here is an example that looks for two different values and assigns two different values:

```
SPL> index=main | top http_uri showperc=false
     | eval Tag=case(http_uri=="/booking/payment", "Payment",
http_uri="/auth", "Authorization")
```

The resulting table shows that a new column called `Tag` has been created and all instances of `/home` have been marked as `Home` and all instances of `/auth` have been marked as `Auth`:

```
index=main | top http_uri showperc=false
    | eval Tag=case(http_uri=="/booking/payment", "Payment", http_uri="/auth", "Authorization")
```

✓ 3,492 events (before 3/8/18 4:59:35.000 PM)   No Event Sampling ∨   Job ∨

| Events | Patterns | Statistics (10) | Visualization |

20 Per Page ∨   ✓ Format   Preview ∨

http_uri ⇕		count ⇕ ✓	Tag ⇕
/auth		276	Authorization
/destination/MCO/details		252	
/destinations/search		251	
/booking/payment		241	Payment

Search command – rex

The rex or regular expression command is extremely useful when you need to extract a field during search time that has not already been extracted automatically. The rex command even works in multi-line events. The following sample command will get all versions of the Chrome browser that are defined in the highlighted user agent string part of the raw data. Let's say this is your raw data, and you need to get the highlighted value:

```
016-07-21 23:58:50:227303,96.32.0.0,GET,/destination/LAX/details,-,80,
-,10.2.1.33,Mozilla/5.0 (Macintosh; Intel Mac OS X 10_8_5)
AppleWebKit/537.36 (KHTML; like Gecko) Chrome/29.0.1547.76
Safari/537.36,500,0,0,823,3053
```

You can use this search command to get it:

```
SPL> index=main | rex field=http_user_agent
     "Chrome/(?<Chrome_Version>.+?)?Safari" | top Chrome_Version
```

The rex command extracted a field called Chrome_Version during the search and made it available for all succeeding commands. The results are shown in the following screenshot:

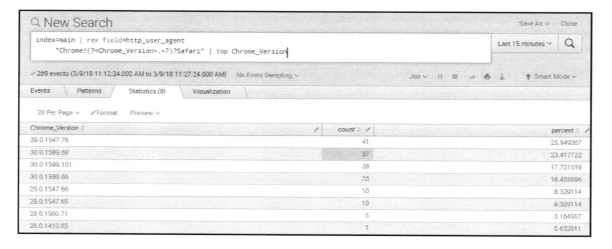

Tip from the Fez: While Splunk allows the `rex` command in SPL, it is generally a best practice—once you're sure that the `rex` command is accurate for your situation—to create a Splunk field extraction so that the regular expression logic can be stored in one place and reused in searches like any other field.

Summary

In this chapter, we introduced you to SPL. You learned that the search pipeline is crucial in the transformation of data as it is piped between search commands and eventually to the final results table. You were introduced to time modifiers to control the timespan of events that searches will consider, and the more commonly used time-range picker. You learned how to filter search results, which happens in almost every Splunk search you'll ever write. Lastly, you were introduced to multiple search commands that are commonly used.

In `Chapter 5`, *Data Optimization, Reports, Alerts, and Accelerating Searches*, we will go on to use our search processing skills to create useful reports, and learn about developing alerts that will increase organizational efficiency and prevent errors. We will also learn more on how to best optimize our searches.

4
Reporting, Alerts, and Search Optimization

Finding the data you need in Splunk is relatively easy, as you have seen in previous chapters. Doing the same thing repeatedly for different datasets, however, requires that you employ techniques that make data retrieval faster, easier, and more controlled with reusable configurations. In Chapter 2, *Bringing in Data*, you were shown how to use data fields and make field extractions. In Chapter 4, *Data Models and Pivot*, you learned how to create data models. You will continue that journey in this chapter by learning how to classify your data using Event Types, enrich your data using Lookups, and normalize your data using Tags.

Once you have these essentials in place, you will be able to more easily create reports, alerts, and dashboards, and capture analytical value from machine data quickly.

In this chapter, we will cover a wide range of topics that showcase ways to manage, analyze, and get results from machine data. These topics will help you work more efficiently with Splunk:

- Data classification with Event Types
- Data normalization with Tags
- Data enrichment with Lookups
- Creating reports
- Creating alerts
- The Custom Cron schedule
- Scheduling options
- Optimizing search performance with acceleration and summaries

Data classification with Event Types

When working with Splunk daily, you will find many of the tasks and searches you run are repeated on a periodic basis. As shown earlier, storing field extraction logic in a single place allows it to be reused in the future. Another way to make things easier and also shorten searches is to create Event Types. Event Types are not the same as events; an event is just a single instance of data. An Event Type is a grouping or classification of events meeting the same search criteria.

If you took a break between chapters, you will probably want to open up Splunk again. Then, execute a search command:

1. Log in to the Splunk portal
2. Click on your **Destinations** app
3. Type this search in the search bar:

```
SPL> index=main http_uri=/booking/confirmation http_status_code=200
```

This search will return events representing successful booking confirmations. In the overall set of requirements, successful bookings is something that most likely will want to be known in a variety of ways, over time. Without any data classification, you'll have to type the same search string as previously entered. Instead of tedious repetition, you can simplify your work by saving the search command as an Event Type. Follow these steps to create some Event Types:

1. In the **Save As** dropdown, select **Event Type**:

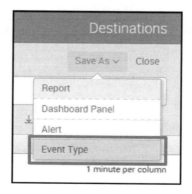

2. Label this new Event Type `good_bookings`.

3. Select a color that is best suited for the type of event; in this case, we will select **green**.

4. Select **5** as the priority. Priority here determines which style wins if there is more than one Event Type. **1** is the highest and **10** is the lowest.

5. Use the following screenshot as a guide, then click on **Save**:

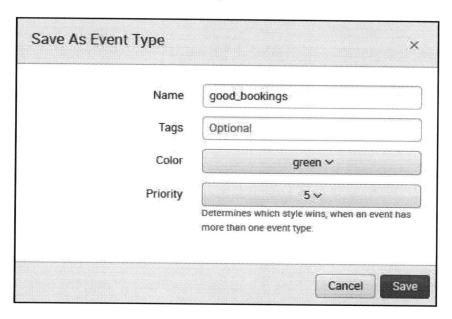

Now, let's create an Event Type for bad bookings:

1. Modify the previous search from `http_status_code=200` to `http_status_code=500`. The new search is as shown here:

```
SPL> index=main http_uri=/booking/confirmation http_status_code=500
```

2. Save this as an Event Type as well. Name it `bad_bookings` and opt for the color to be **red**, leaving **Priority** as **5**:

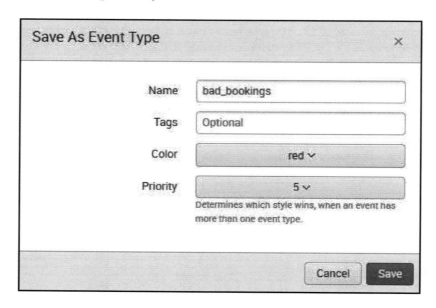

We have created two Event Types. Let's see them in action:

1. Enter the following search:

   SPL> eventtype=*bookings

2. The results should appear similar to the following screenshot. Notice that the search results have now been colored based on the assigned Event Type, making it easy to spot either of the two types of booking. You can also search for eventtype=good_bookings or eventtype=bad_bookings to narrow the search results:

i	Time	Event
	1/31/18 2:48:41.363 PM	2018-01-31 14:48:41:363363,166.56.0.0,GET,/booking/confirmation,-,80,-,10.2.1.33,Mozilla/5.0 (X11; Linux i686) AppleWebKit/537.36 (KHTML; like Gecko) Chrome/29.0.1547.76 Safari/537.36,500,0,0,538,1009 host = www.destinations.com ⁞ source = web_log ⁞ sourcetype = access_custom
	1/31/18 2:47:11.440 PM	2018-01-31 14:47:11:440697,167.67.0.0,GET,/booking/confirmation,-,80,-,10.2.1.35,Mozilla/5.0 (X11; Linux x86_64; rv:24.0) Gecko/201 00101 Firefox/24.0,500,0,0,380,1661 host = www.destinations.com ⁞ source = web_log ⁞ sourcetype = access_custom
	1/31/18 2:46:43.235 PM	2018-01-31 14:46:43:235635,169.38.0.0,GET,/booking/confirmation,-,80,-,10.2.1.35,Mozilla/5.0 (Windows NT 6.0) AppleWebKit/537.36 (K HTML; like Gecko) Chrome/29.0.1547.76 Safari/537.36,200,0,0,297,2880 host = www.destinations.com ⁞ source = web_log ⁞ sourcetype = access_custom
	1/31/18 2:43:53.039 PM	2018-01-31 14:43:53:039253,132.190.0.0,GET,/booking/confirmation,-,80,-,10.2.1.35,Mozilla/5.0 (Macintosh; Intel Mac OS X 10.7; rv:2 4.0) Gecko/20100101 Firefox/24.0,200,0,0,122,488 host = www.destinations.com ⁞ source = web_log ⁞ sourcetype = access_custom
	1/31/18 2:42:07.242 PM	2018-01-31 14:42:07:242629,158.91.0.0,GET,/booking/confirmation,-,80,-,10.2.1.35,Mozilla/5.0 (Windows NT 5.1; rv:23.0) Gecko/201001 01 Firefox/23.0,200,0,0,611,1863 host = www.destinations.com ⁞ source = web_log ⁞ sourcetype = access_custom
	1/31/18 2:40:56.101 PM	2018-01-31 14:40:56:101656,209.211.0.0,GET,/booking/confirmation,-,80,-,10.2.1.34,Mozilla/5.0 (Windows NT 6.1) AppleWebKit/537.36 (KHTML; like Gecko) Chrome/30.0.1599.66 Safari/537.36,500,0,0,926,2485 host = www.destinations.com ⁞ source = web_log ⁞ sourcetype = access_custom

TIP

Certain restrictions apply when creating Event Types. You cannot create an `eventtype` that consists of a piped command or subsearches. Only base commands can be saved as an Event Type.

Since the `eventtype` is now part of the search, you can add more search logic using piped commands, for example:

```
SPL> eventtype=*bookings | stats count by eventtype
```

Create a few more Event Types using the following table as a guide. After modifying the search command, you must execute the search for the Event Type to be saved accurately. Set all Priorities to **5** when creating the four Event Types as given in the following table:

Event Type	Search command	Color
good_payment	index=main http_uri=/booking/payment http_status_code=200	**green**
bad_payment	index=main http_uri=/booking/payment http_status_code=500	**red**
destination_details	index=main http_uri=/destination/*/details	**blue**
bad_logins	index=main http_uri=/auth http_status_code=500	**purple**

Data normalization with Tags

Tags in Splunk are useful for grouping events with related field values. Unlike Event Types, which are based on specified search commands, Tags are created and mapped to specific field-value combinations. Multiple Tags can be assigned to the same field-value combination.

A common scenario of using Tags is for classifying IP addresses. In the Eventgen logs, three IP addresses are automatically generated. We will create Tags against these IP addresses to allow us to classify them:

IP address	Tags
10.2.1.33	main, patched, and east
10.2.1.34	main, patched, and west
10.2.1.35	backup and east

We are going to group IP addresses by purpose, patch status, and geolocation in the server farm of three servers represented in our Eventgen data. We will achieve this using Tags, as shown in the following steps:

1. Begin by using the following search command:

   ```
   SPL> index=main server_ip=10.2.1.33
   ```

2. Expand the first event by clicking on the information field, as seen in this screenshot:

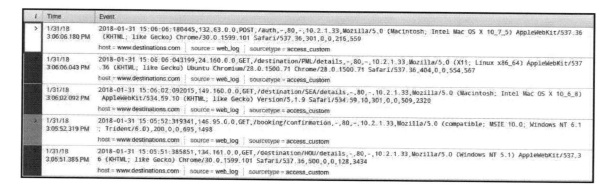

3. While expanded, look for the **server_ip** field. Click on the **Actions** dropdown and select **Edit Tags**:

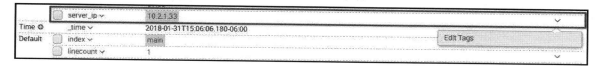

4. In the **Create Tags** window, fill in the **Tag(s)** text area using the following screenshot as a guide. For `10.2.1.33`, you will use the following Tags: `main`, `patched`, and `east`.

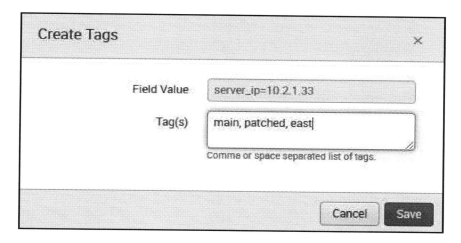

5. Click on **Save** when you're done.

6. Do the same for the remaining two IP addresses and create Tags based on the previous table.

7. To see Tags in action, run the following search command:

```
SPL> index=main tag=patched OR tag=east
```

This will give you all the events that come from the servers that are patched or located in the east. You can then combine these with other search commands or an Event Type to narrow down the search results.

Consider a scenario where you need to find all booking payments with errors originating from the servers in east.

Without Event Types or Tags, you would create a search command such as:

```
SPL> index=main server_ip=10.2.1.33 OR server_ip=10.2.1.35
     AND (http_uri=/booking/payment http_status_code=500)
```

Compare that to this much more elegant and shorter search command:

```
SPL> eventtype=bad_payment tag=east
```

Here's an additional exercise for you. Create Tags for the following fields using this table as a guide and use them in a search query. Remember to begin your search with `index=main` and then the field and value, to get the correct results to apply the Tag:

Field and value	Tags
http_uri = /destination/LAX/details	major_destination
http_uri = /destination/NY/details	major_destination
http_uri = /destination/MIA/details	home
http_status_code = 301	redirect
http_status_code = 404	not_found

Now, you can use these Tags to search for bookings to major destinations that have a status code Tag of `not_found`. Here is an example of a search command that combines what you have learned in this chapter so far:

- Go ahead and run this now:

```
SPL> eventtype=destination_details tag=major_destination
     tag=not_found
```

- Look through your results and see that you now have data from the destinations LAX and NY, where the response code indicates the page was not found.

Data enrichment with Lookups

Occasionally you will require pieces of data to be rendered in a more readable manner. A common example to go through using our Eventgen data is with HTTP status. Computer engineers are often familiar with HTTP status codes as three-digit numbers. Business analysts or more casual users may not know the meaning of these codes and require a text-based description to comprehend the search results. In Splunk, you can enrich event data using Lookups, which can pair numbers or acronyms with more understandable text descriptions found in a separate file.

A lookup table is a mapping of keys and values Splunk can search, allowing for the displaying of more meaningful information at search time. Having the Lookup execute at search run time also optimizes the need to index verbose descriptions that consume additional index space. This is best understood through an example:

1. From the **Destinations** app, click on **Settings** and then **Lookups**:

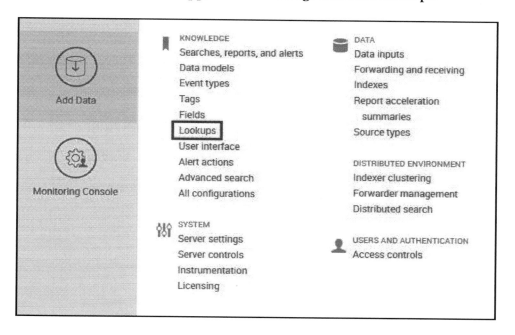

2. In the **Lookups** page, click on the **Add new** option next to **Lookup table files**, as shown in the following screenshot:

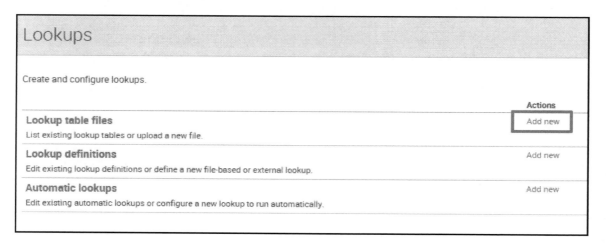

3. In the **Add new** page, make sure that the **Destinations** app is selected
4. Then, using the following screenshot as your guide, in **Upload a lookup file**, browse and choose the following: `C:\splunk-essentials-master\labs\chapter05\http_status.csv`
5. Finally, type in `http_status.csv` in the **Destination filename** field
6. Click on **Save** to complete:

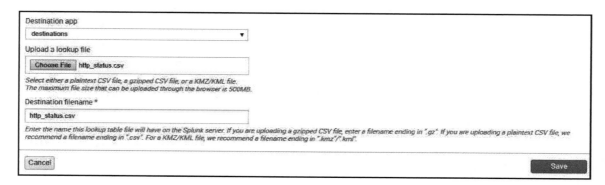

The new Lookup table file path will now appear in the **Lookup Table Files** page. Change the permission so that all apps can use it and it will now appear as **Global**. The entries in the Lookup table files should be similar to the following screenshot:

Now that we have told Splunk where to access the Lookup file, it is time to create the Lookup definition:

1. In the **Lookups** page, click on the **Add new** option next to **Lookup definitions**:

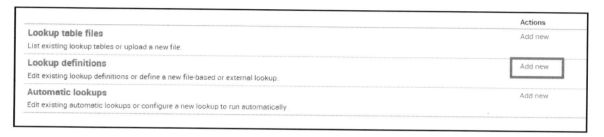

2. Once again, make sure that this is being saved in the context of the **Destinations** app.
3. In the name field, type in `http_status`.
4. Leave the **Type** as **File-based**. In the **Lookup file** dropdown, look for the **http_status.csv** file and select it.
5. Leave the remaining checkboxes blank:

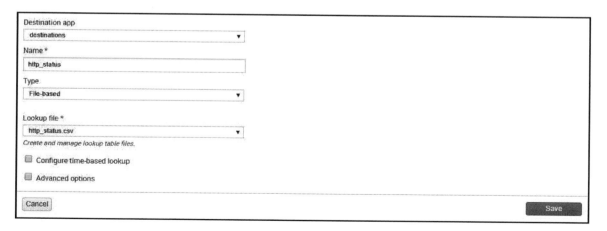

6. Save the definition.
7. The new Lookup definition will now appear in the Lookup definitions page. Change permission sharing to **Global** by allowing **All Apps** to have permissions, and assign **Read** access to **Everyone** and **Write** access to the **admin** user.

To now use the new Lookup:

1. In the **Destinations** app search bar, type in:

   ```
   SPL> eventtype=destination_details | top http_status_code
   ```

2. The result will show the `http_status_code` column with the raw status code values, as well as the counts and percentage of total for each. Extend the search by using the `lookup` command:

   ```
   SPL> eventtype=destination_details
                     | top http_status_code
                     | rename http_status_code AS status
                     | lookup http_status status OUTPUT
                       status_description, status_type
   ```

3. Look at the following output. The steps you took give you a meaningful output showing the description and type of the status codes by using the Lookup:

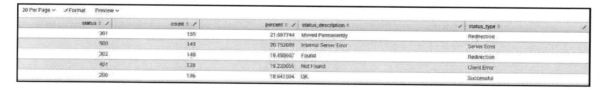

status	count	percent	status_description	status_type
301	155	21.587744	Moved Permanently	Redirection
500	149	20.752089	Internal Server Error	Server Error
302	140	19.498607	Found	Redirection
404	138	19.220056	Not Found	Client Error
200	136	18.941504	OK	Successful

Adding the Lookup is good for a first step, but for it to be repetitively used by casual users, the Lookup needs to happen automatically when searches including `http_status_code` are run. To do this, take the following steps:

1. Go back to **Settings** and then the **Lookups** page.
2. Click on **Add new** next to **Automatic Lookups**:

3. Complete the form with the following information. Leaving the second column under Lookup output fields blank defaults the display name of the fields to what is in the file. Click on **Save** when you're done:

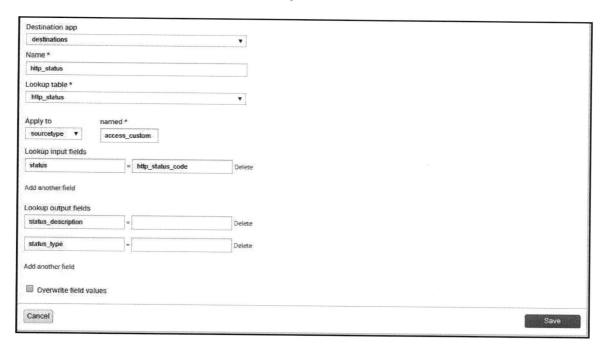

4. Click on **Permissions** and change the sharing permission to **Global** by clicking on **All Apps**, giving everyone **Read** access and admins **Write** access; then click on **Save**.

Let's see how these changes help:

1. Go back to the **Destinations** app search bar and type in the following search:

   ```
   SPL> eventtype=destination_details status_type=Redirection
   ```

   You have now filtered your search using values from the Lookup information without invoking the `lookup` command explicitly in the SPL.

2. Notice that the search output will match all events where `http_status_code` equals `301` or `302`.

 Tip from the Fez: If there are values in the raw event data without a corresponding match in the `lookup` file, they will be dropped by default when summarizing by Lookup values. Visit the Splunk documentation for additional options available when using Lookups.

Creating and scheduling reports

In this chapter, you have learned three very important things: classifying raw events using Event Types, classifying data using Tags, and enriching data using Lookups. These, in addition to good SPL, constitute essential elements you need to use Splunk in an efficient manner.

Splunk reports are saved searches which can be shared to others or used as a dashboard panel. Reports can be scheduled periodically and perform an action upon completion, such as sending an email with the report results.

Reports can be configured to display search results in a statistical table, as well as visualization charts. A report is created using the search command line or through a Pivot. Here we will create a report using the search command line:

1. In the **Destinations** app's search page, run the following search:

   ```
   SPL> eventtype=bad_logins | top client_ip
   ```

   The search delivers results for the top 10 client IP addresses that attempted to authenticate but got a 500 internal server error.

2. To save this as a report for the future, go to **Save As** | **Report** and then give it the title `Bad Logins`:

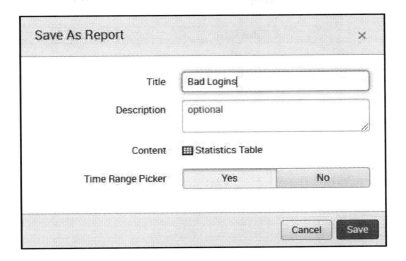

3. Next, click on **Save**.
4. Then click on **View** to go back to the search results.
5. Notice that the report is now properly labeled with our title. You can see an example of the report in the following screenshot:

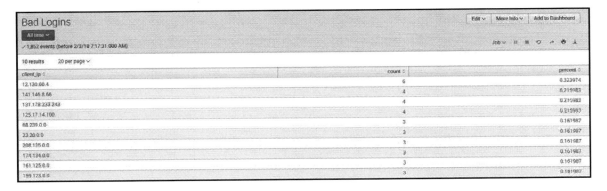

6. Expanding the **Edit** dropdown, you will see additional options to consider while working on this report.

You can modify the permissions so that others can use your report. You have done this step a couple of times earlier in the book. This process will be identical to editing permissions for other objects in Splunk.

You can create a schedule to run this report on a timely basis and perform an action on it. Unfortunately, you'll need a mail server to send an email, so you may not be able to do this from your Splunk workstation. However, we will show the steps to schedule a report and take action upon completion:

1. Go to **Edit | Edit Schedule**.
2. In the **Edit Schedule** window, click on the **Schedule Report** checkbox.
3. Change the **Schedule** option to run **Every Day**. The time range applies to the search time scope.

   Schedule windows are important for production environments. The schedule window you specify should be less than the time range. When there are multiple concurrent searches going on in the Splunk system, it will check whether you have a schedule window and delay your report up to the defined time, or until no other concurrent searches are running. This is one way of optimizing your Splunk system. If you need accurate results that are based on your time range, however, do not use the schedule window option.

   Schedule priority refers to the preference of running scheduled reports before other reports of a lower priority, which becomes important if a variety of reports are all scheduled to run at the same time.

4. Refer to the following screenshot; then, click on **Next** when you're ready to move on:

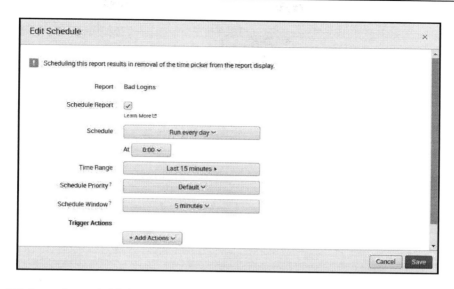

5. Click on the **+ Add Actions** and select the **Send email** to show advanced email options. Once again, since your workstation does not have a mail server, the scheduled report will not work. But it is worth viewing what the advanced email options look like:

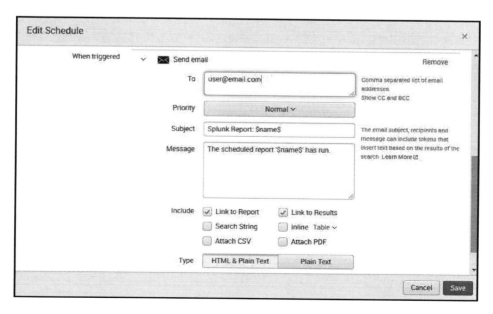

6. Remove the **Send Email** option and click on **Save**. The report will still run, but it will not perform the email action.

Another option commonly used for reports is adding them as dashboard panels. You can do this with the **Add to Dashboard** button. We will use this option in Chapter 6, *Panes of Glass*.

Create a few more reports from SPL using the following guidelines. We will use some of these reports in future chapters, so try your best to do all of them. You can always come back to this chapter if you need to:

Search	Schedule	Report name	Time range	Schedule window
`eventtype=bad_payment	top client_ip`	Run every hour	Bad payments	Last 24 hrs	30 mins
`eventtype=good_bookings	timechart span=1h count`	Run every day	Bookings last 24 hrs	Last 24 hrs	15 mins

You also have the ability to create reports using Pivot:

1. Click on **Datasets**.
2. Create a Pivot table on the **Destinations | WebLogs | Destination Details** child object with **Last 24 hours** as your **Filters** and **Airport Code** as your **Split Rows**. See this screenshot to confirm your selections:

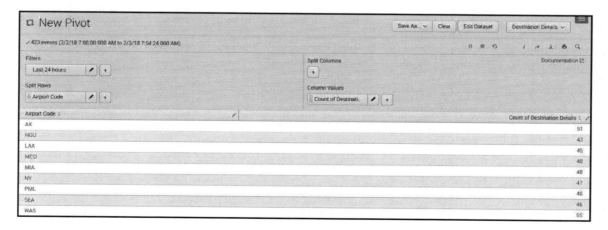

3. Save the pivot as a report titled `Destinations by Airport Code`. Schedule the report to run every hour, within a 24-hour time range, and with a 30-minute time window.

We will return to use these reports later in the book.

Creating alerts

Alerts are crucial in IT and security operations. They provide proactive awareness of the state of the systems to those persons who monitor and control them. Alerts enable you to act fast when an issue has been detected, as opposed to waiting for a user to run a report and find the issue, which may or may not happen. In today's world, every minute someone has breached your network is costly and potentially devastating.

However, alerts are only good if they are controlled and if they provide enough actionable information. They should not be created on low-priority items or triggered too often to the point they lose relevance.

Tip from the Fez: Out-of-the box functionality for alerts is most commonly driven to email. Users may also want to explore the use of text messages. When Splunk doesn't provide something out of the box, there is a good chance the Splunk community has filled the gap. Consider the use of the Twilio SMS Alerting add-on found on Splunkbase at `https://splunkbase.splunk.com/app/2865/` or explore other various comments and suggestions on Splunk answers.

In this example, we want to know when there are instances of a failed booking scenario. This Event Type was constructed with the 500 HTTP status code. 5xx status codes are the most devastating errors in a web application so we want to be aware of them. We will create an alert to be triggered when a bad booking event occurs. Follow these steps:

1. To create the alert, run the following search, while updating the time-range picker to Last 60 minutes:

```
SPL> eventtype=bad_bookings
```

2. Click on **Save As** | **Alert**. In the **Save As Alert** window, fill up the form using the following screenshot as a guide:

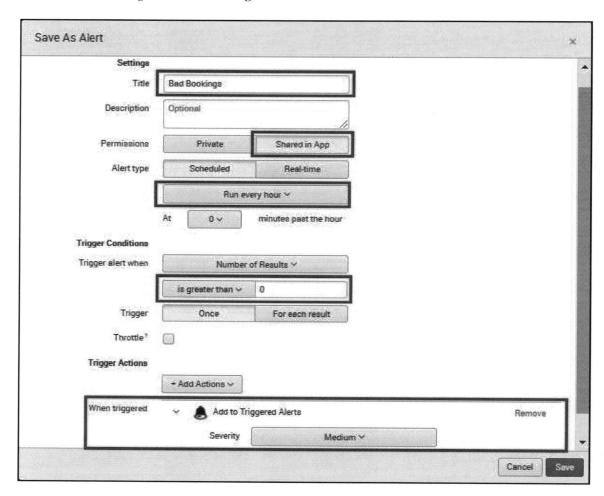

Here is an explanation of different options in this window:

- **Permissions**: You should be fairly familiar with permissions by now. These apply to alerts as well.
- **Alert type**: There are two ways to create an alert, just as there are two ways to run a search: scheduled (ad hoc) or in real time. Splunk has predefined schedules that you can easily use, namely:
  - Run every hour.
  - Run every day.
  - Run every week.
  - Run every month.
  - Although the preceding schedules are convenient, you will likely soon find yourself wanting more granularity for your searches. This is where the fifth option comes in: **Run on Cron** schedule. We will discuss this in detail later in the chapter.
- **Trigger Conditions**: These are the conditions or rules that define when the alert will be generated. The predefined conditions that Splunk offers out of the box are:
  - **Number of Results**: Most commonly used, this tells the alert to run whenever your search returns a certain number of events
  - **Number of Hosts**: This is used when you need to know how many hosts are returning events based on your search
  - **Number of Sources**: This is used when you need to know how many data sources are returning events based on your search
  - **Custom**: This is used when you want to base your condition on the value of a particular field that is returned in your search result
- **Trigger Actions**: These are the actions that will be invoked when your trigger conditions are met. There are several possible default trigger actions currently included in Splunk Enterprise:
  - **Add to Triggered Alerts**: This will add an entry to the **Activity** | **Triggered alerts** page. This is what we will use in this book since it is an option contained within Splunk.
  - **Log Event**: Send the event to a Splunk receiver, such as a forwarder or another Splunk Enterprise server.
  - **Output Results to Lookup**: Rather than sending events to another Splunk receiver in the prior example, this selection places the results in a Lookup table which can be captured from your Splunk server or searched in Splunk using the Lookup functionality we covered earlier in this chapter.

- **Run a script**: You can run a script (such as a Powershell, Linux Shell, or Python script) located in the $SPLUNK_HOME/bin/scripts directory whenever this alert is generated. This functionality can be helpful for self-repairing or remote shutdown tasks to be taken upon a trigger.
- **Send e-mail**: Commonly used but requires a mail server to be configured.
- **Webhook**: Allows Splunk to make an HTTP POST to an external application.
- **Manage Actions:** Valuable in this selection is the ability to browse for more actions. While not included in the out-of-the-box Splunk package, there are suggestions for additional actions possible with prebuilt Splunk add-ons. After the alert, common tasks could be to create incidents and events in IT Service Management tools such as ServiceNow, or send messages via instant message tools such as Slack.

Click on **Save** to save your first alert. If you are using a Splunk Enterprise trial license, you may receive a warning about the alert not working after the trial completes. While it is important to note the warning, click on **View Alert** to get to the alert details screen for the **Booking Errors** alert.

The alert details page allows you to continue to make changes if needed. Note that since we selected the **Add to Triggered Alerts** action, you should now see the history of when this alert was triggered on your machine. Since the Eventgen data is randomized and we scheduled it to run every hour at the beginning of the hour, you may have to wait until the next hour for results:

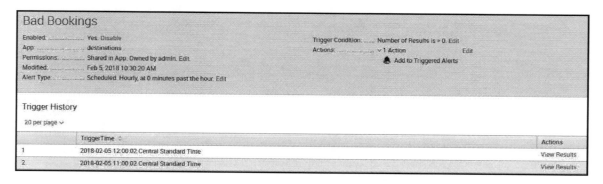

Search and Report acceleration

In `Chapter 4`, *Data Models and Pivot*, you learned how to accelerate a data model to speed up retrieval of data. The same principle applies to saved searches or reports:

1. Click on the **Reports** link in the navigation menu of the **Destinations** app
2. Click on the **Edit | Edit Acceleration** option in the **Bookings Last 24 Hrs** report:

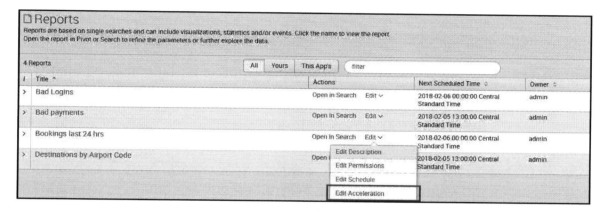

3. Enable **1 Day** acceleration as seen in the following screenshot and click on **Save**:

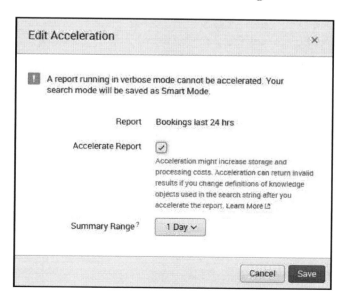

4. To check the progress of your report's acceleration, click on **Settings** | **Report acceleration summaries**:

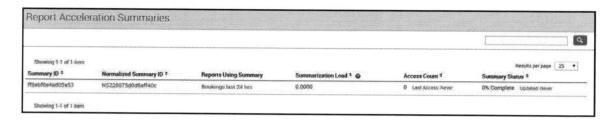

 If Eventgen has not been running for more than a day, the report acceleration build may not execute because there is not enough data for the scope of the acceleration. To verify the report acceleration, ensure that Eventgen has been running.

Scheduling options

No matter how advanced and well-scaled your Splunk infrastructure is, if all scheduled reports and alerts are running at the same time, the system will start experiencing performance issues. Typically, you will receive a Splunk message saying that you have reached the limit of concurrent or historical searches. There are only a certain number of searches that can be run on fixed CPU capacity for each Splunk server or collection of servers. A common problem a Splunk administrator will inevitably face is how to limit the number of searches running at the same time. One way to fix this is to throw more servers into you Splunk environment, but that is not a cost-efficient way.

It is important to properly stagger and plan scheduled searches, reports, alerts, dashboards, and so on, ensuring they are not all running at the same time. In addition to the schedule time, there are two ways to help achieve staggering in scheduled search runs:

- **Time windows**: The first way to ensure that searches are not running concurrently is to set a time window. You have done this in the exercises in this chapter. This is not ideal if you need to schedule searches for an exact time.
- **Custom Cron schedule**: This is what most advanced users use to create their schedules. Cron is a system daemon, or a computer program that runs as a background process, derived from traditional UNIX systems, and is used to execute tasks at specified times.

Let's go through an example of how to use a Custom Cron schedule. Begin with this search in the **Destinations** app search bar, which finds all errors in a payment:

1. Enter and run the following search:

   ```
   SPL> eventtype=bad_payment
   ```

2. Save it as an alert by clicking on **Save As | Alert**.
3. Name it Payment Errors.
4. Change the permissions to Shared in App.
5. In the **Alert type**, change the schedule to **Run on Cron Schedule**.
6. Click on the **Time Range** button to access a slimmed-down version of the time-range picker.
7. On the **Relative** tab, in the **Earliest** field, enter 15 and change the drop-down selection to **Minutes Ago**. Also select **Beginning of minute** to ensure it starts at the beginning of the 15th minute.
8. For **Latest**, leave the default selection of **Now**.
9. Click on **Apply** to return to the **Save As Alert** window. Not clicking on the **Apply** button will mean your recent entries will not be saved for use.
10. In the **Cron Expression** field, leave the default entry, but be sure to see the next table for a clear explanation of what the Cron expression options are.

11. Finally, change the **Trigger Actions** to **Add to Triggered Alerts**. Use the following screenshot as a guide:

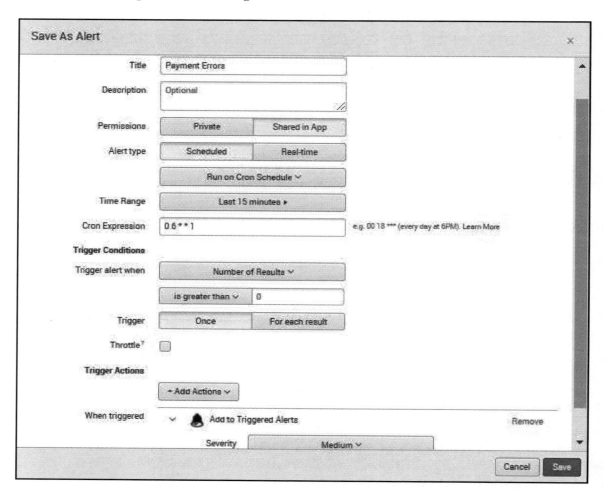

12. Click on **Save** when done.

The Cron expression * * * * * corresponds to minute, hour, day, month, day-of-week.

Learning Cron expressions is easiest when you look at examples. The more examples, the simpler it is to understand this method of scheduling. Here are some typical examples:

Cron expression	Schedule
*/5 * * * *	Every 5 minutes
*/15 * * * *	Every 15 minutes
0 */6 * * *	Every 6 hours, on the hour
30 */2 * * *	Every 2 hours at the 30th minute (for instance, 3:30)
45 14 1,10 * *	Every 1st and 10th of the month, at 2:45 pm.
0 */1 * 1-5	Every hour, Monday to Friday
2,17,32,47 * * * *	Every 2nd minute, 17th minute, 32nd minute, and 47th minute of every hour.

Now that you know something about Cron expressions, you can fine-tune all your searches to run in precise and different schedules.

Summary indexing

In a matter of days, Splunk will accumulate data and start to move events through the bucketing process. With the millions or billions of events that are typical with a robust Splunk implementation, you can start to understand how searches run over long-time horizons can slow down.

There are two ways to circumvent this problem. In addition to search acceleration, completed earlier in this chapter, faster search results on large amounts of data can be achieved through summary indexing.

With summary indexing, you run a scheduled search and output the results into a different index, often called **summary**. The result will only show the computed statistics of the search. This results in a very small subset of data that will be much faster to retrieve and report on than going through a large set of detailed event records and summarizing results on the fly. This concept is not unlike the notion of creating aggregate tables or pre-calculated views in a relational database management system, where data is pre-calculated and results stored for access at some point in the future.

Say, for example, you wish to keep track of payment error counts and you wish to keep the data in the summary index. Follow these steps:

1. From your **Destinations** app, go to **Settings | Searches, reports, and alerts**.
2. Click on the **New Report** button to create a new scheduled search.
3. Use the following information as a guide:
   - **Title**: Summary of Payment Errors
   - **Search**: eventtype=bad_payment | stats count
   - **Earliest time**: -2m@m
   - **Latest time**: now
   - **App**: Destinations
   - **Time Range Picker**: No
4. Click on **Save** when complete. Use the following screenshot as a guide:

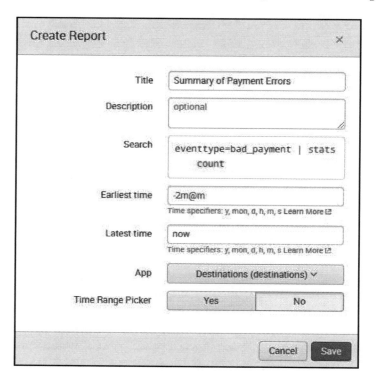

Now, perform the following steps:

1. Click on the **Edit** drop-down menu next to the report you just created and select **Edit Schedule**
2. Change **Schedule type** to **Cron**
3. Set **Cron schedule** to */2 * * * *
4. Click on **Save**

Use the following screenshot as a guide:

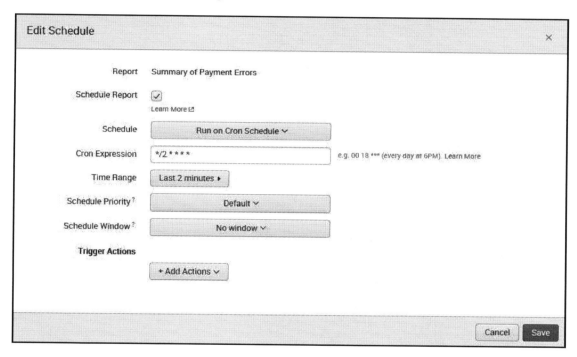

Now perform the following steps:

1. Again, click on the **Edit** drop-down menu for the report and select **Edit Summary indexing**.
2. Check the box to start the process of enabling summary indexing.
3. Add a new field in the **Add fields** section, where values will be summaryCount equals to count.

Use the following information as a guide:

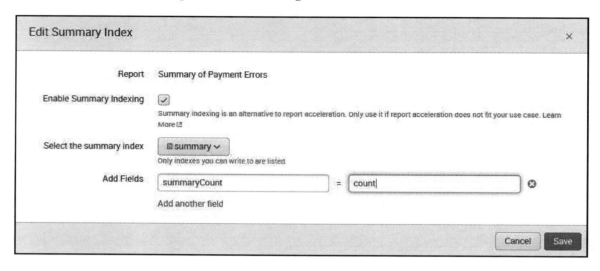

4. Save when you are ready to continue.
5. Wait just a few minutes, and then go back to the **Destinations** app's search page. Type in and execute the following search:

```
SPL> index=summary search_name="Summary of Payment Errors" | table
_time,count
```

The statistics tab will appear first when showing the results of the search, due to the `table` command. Clicking on the **Events** table will show the events loaded into the summary index. Notice these events are stripped of the original event fields. Also notice that even if there were zero results returned during the two minute window, an event is stored with **count=0**. We will use this information in later chapters to create optimized dashboards.

Summary

In this chapter, you learned how to enhance data in three ways: classifying data using Event Types, normalizing data using Tags, and enriching data using Lookups. You also learned some reporting and alerting techniques, along with report acceleration. You were introduced to the powerful Cron expression, which allows you to create granularity on your scheduled searches, as well as stagger execution times. Finally, you were introduced to the concept of summary indexing, allowing searches against pre-aggregated and stored historical data in the interest of performance.

In the next chapter, Chapter 6, *Panes of Glass*, you will go on to learn how to do visualizations.

5
Dynamic Dashboarding

Splunk makes it easy to visualize many different KPIs or reports in a single view using its dashboard functionality. For users to adopt the dashboard, it must be fast, easy to use, and carefully laid out to answer a variety of common queries. Splunk comes with a wide variety of chart types to visually represent your data, as you've seen in prior exercises in this book. Charts and reports can be organized into a dashboard layout with minimal effort. With practice, you can spin off a dashboard in a fraction of the time it would take if you were writing custom software to accomplish the same task.

In this chapter, we will cover the following topics:

- Identifying different types of dashboards
- Gathering business requirements for your dashboard
- Modifying dashboard panels
- Building multi-panel, dynamic dashboards showing relevant key performance indicators

Creating effective dashboards

Splunk is easy to use for developing a powerful analytical dashboard with multiple panels. A dashboard with too many panels, however, will require scrolling down the page and can cause the viewer to miss crucial information. An effective dashboard should generally meet the following conditions:

- **Single screen view**: The dashboard fits in a single window or page, with no scrolling
- **Multiple data points**: Charts and visualizations should display a number of data points

- **Crucial information highlighted**: The dashboard points out the most important information, using appropriate titles, labels, legends, markers, and conditional formatting as required
- **Created with the user in mind**: Data is presented in a way that is meaningful to the user
- **Loads quickly**: The dashboard returns results in 10 seconds or less
- **Avoid redundancy**: The display does not repeat information in multiple places

Types of dashboards

There are three kinds of dashboards typically created with Splunk:

- Dynamic form-based dashboards
- Real-time dashboards
- Dashboards as scheduled reports

Dynamic form-based dashboards allow Splunk users to modify the dashboard data without leaving the page. This is accomplished by adding data-driven input fields (such as time, radio button, textbox, checkbox, dropdown, and so on) to the dashboard. Updating these inputs changes the data based on the selections. Dynamic form-based dashboards have existed in traditional business intelligence tools for decades now, so users who frequently use them will be familiar with changing prompt values on the fly to update the dashboard data.

Real-time dashboards are often kept on a big panel screen for constant viewing, simply because they are so useful. You see these dashboards in data centers, **network operations centers** (**NOCs**), or **security operations centers** (**SOCs**) with constant format and data changing in real time. The dashboard will also have indicators and alerts for operators to easily identify and act on a problem. Dashboards like this typically show the current state of security, network, or business systems, using indicators for web performance and traffic, revenue flow, login failures, and other important measures.

Dashboards as scheduled reports may not be exposed for viewing; however, the dashboard view will generally be saved as a PDF file and sent to email recipients at scheduled times. This format is ideal when you need to send information updates to multiple recipients at regular intervals, and don't want to force them to log in to Splunk to capture the information themselves.

In this chapter, we will create the first two types of dashboards, and you will learn how to use the Splunk dashboard editor to develop advanced visualizations along the way.

Gathering business requirements

As a Splunk administrator, one of the most important responsibilities is to be responsible for the data. As a custodian of data, a Splunk admin has significant influence over how to interpret and present information to users. It is common for the administrator to create the first few dashboards. A more mature implementation, however, requires collaboration to create an output that is beneficial to a variety of user requirements, and may be completed by a Splunk development resource with limited administrative rights.

Make it a habit to consistently request users input regarding the Splunk delivered dashboards and reports and what makes them useful. Sit down with day-to-day users and lay out, on a drawing board for example, the business process flows or system diagrams to understand how the underlying processes and systems you're trying to measure really work. Look for key phrases like these, which signify what data is most important to the business:

- *If this is broken, we lose tons of revenue...*
- *This is a constant point of failure...*
- *We don't know what's going on here...*
- *If only I can see the trend, it will make my work easier...*
- *This is what my boss wants to see...*

Splunk dashboard users may come from many areas of the business. You want to talk to all the different users, no matter where they are on the organizational chart. When you make friends with the architects, developers, business analysts, and management, you will end up building dashboards that benefit the organization, not just individuals. With an initial dashboard version, ask for users thoughts as you observe them using it in their work and ask what can be improved upon, added, or changed.

We hope that at this point, you realize the importance of dashboards and are ready to get started creating some, as we will do in the following sections.

Dynamic form-based dashboard

In this section, we will create a dynamic form-based dashboard in our **Destinations** app to allow users to change input values and rerun the dashboard, presenting updated data. Here is a screenshot of the final output of this dynamic form-based dashboard:

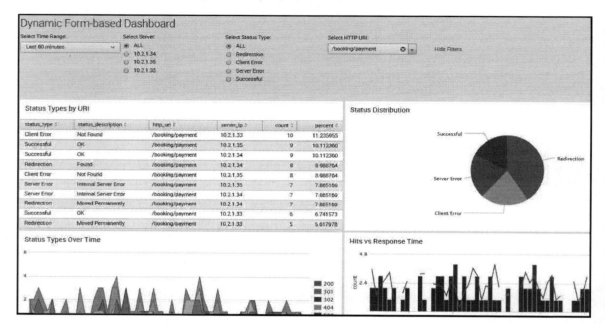

Dynamic dashboard with form input

Let's begin by creating the dashboard itself and then generate the panels:

1. Go the search bar in the **Destinations** app
2. Run this search command:

```
SPL> index=main status_type="*" http_uri="*" server_ip="*"
        | top status_type, status_description, http_uri,
server_ip
```

 Be careful when copying commands with quotation marks. It is best to type in the entire search command to avoid problems.

3. Go to **Save As | Dashboard Panel**
4. Fill in the information based on the following screenshot:

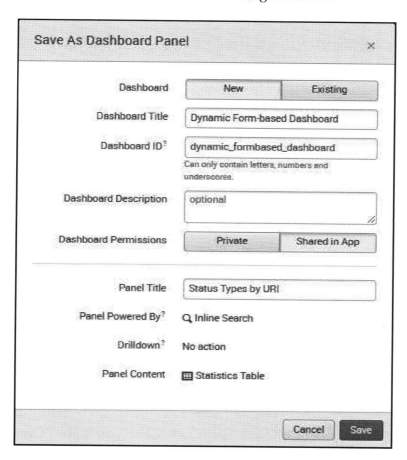

5. Click on **Save**
6. Close the pop-up window that appears (indicating that the dashboard panel was created) by clicking on the **X** in the top-right corner of the window

Creating a Status Distribution panel

We will go to the after all the panel searches have been generated. Let's go ahead and create the second panel:

1. In the search window, type in the following search command:

    ```
    SPL> index=main status_type="*" http_uri=* server_ip=*
         | top status_type
    ```

2. You will save this as a dashboard panel in the newly created dashboard. In the **Dashboard** option, click on the **Existing** button and look for the new dashboard, as seen here. Don't forget to fill in the **Panel Title** as Status Distribution:

3. Click on **Save** when you are done and again close the pop-up window, signaling the addition of the panel to the dashboard.

Creating the Status Types Over Time panel

Now, we'll move on to create the third panel:

1. Type in the following search command and be sure to run it so that it is the active search:

   ```
   SPL> index=main status_type="*" http_uri=* server_ip=*
          | timechart count by http_status_code
   ```

2. You will save this as a Dynamic Form-based Dashboard panel as well. Type in Status Types Over Time in the **Panel Title** field:

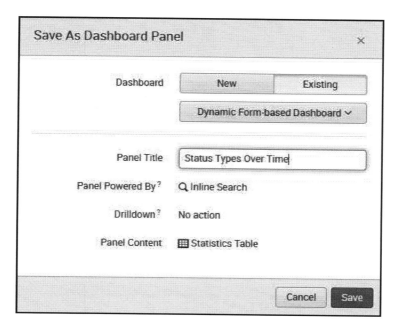

3. Click on **Save** and close the pop-up window, signaling the addition of the panel to the dashboard.

Creating the Hits vs Response Time panel

Now, on to the final panel. Run the following search command:

```
SPL> index=main status_type="*" http_uri=* server_ip=*
     | timechart count, avg(http_response_time) as response_time
```

Save this dashboard panel as Hits vs Response Time:

Arrange the dashboard

We'll move on to look at the dashboard we've created and make a few changes:

1. Click on the **View Dashboard** button. If you missed out on the **View Dashboard** button, you can find your dashboard by clicking on **Dashboards** in the main navigation bar.
2. Let's edit the panel arrangement. Click on the **Edit** button.
3. Move the **Status Distribution** panel to the upper-right row.
4. Move the **Hits vs Response Time** panel to the lower-right row.
5. Click on **Save** to save your layout changes.

Look at the following screenshot. The dashboard framework you've created should now look much like this.

The dashboard probably looks a little plainer than you expected it to. But don't worry; we will improve the dashboard visuals one panel at a time:

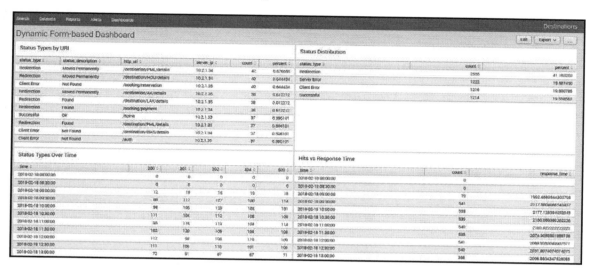

Dynamic dashboard with four panels in tabular format

Panel options

In this section, we will learn how to alter the look of our panels and create visualizations.

Go to the edit dashboard mode by clicking on the **Edit** button.

Each dashboard panel will have three setting options to work with: **edit search**, **select visualization**, and **visualization format** options. They are represented by three drop-down icons:

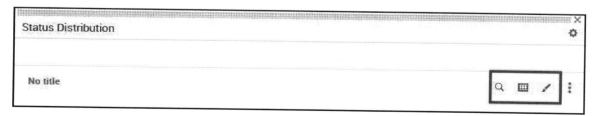

The **Edit Search** window allows you to modify the search string, change the time modifier for the search, add auto-refresh and progress bar options, as well as convert the panel into a report:

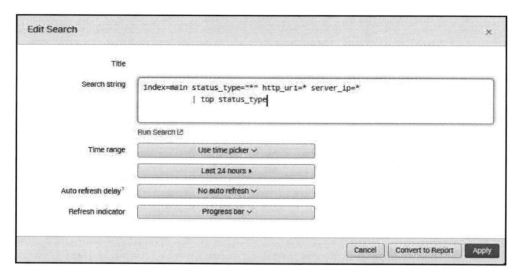

The **Select Visualization** dropdown allows you to change the type of visualization to use for the panel, as shown in the following screenshot:

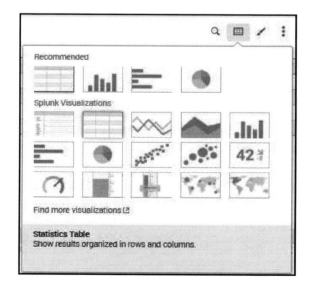

Finally, the **Visualization Options** dropdown will give you the ability to fine-tune your visualization. These options will change depending on the visualization you select. For a normal statistics table, this is how it will look:

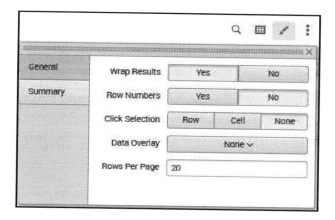

Pie chart – Status Distribution

Go ahead and change the **Status Distribution** visualization panel to a pie chart. You do this by selecting the **Select Visualization** icon and selecting the **Pie** icon. Once done, the panel will look like the following screenshot:

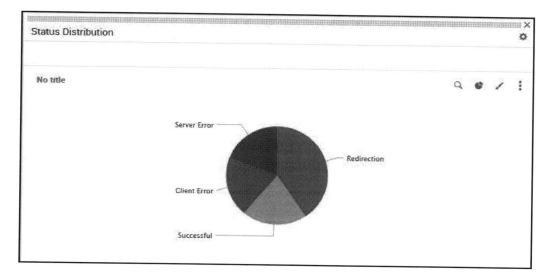

Stacked area chart – Status Types Over Time

We will change the view of the **Status Types Over Time** panel to an area chart. However, by default, area charts will not be stacked. We will update this through adjusting the visualization options:

1. Change the **Status Types Over Time** panel to an **Area** Chart using the same **Select Visualization** button as the prior pie chart exercise.
2. Make the area chart stacked using the **Format Visualization** icon. In the **Stack Mode** section, click on **Stacked**. For **Null Values**, select **Zero**. Use the chart that follows for guidance:

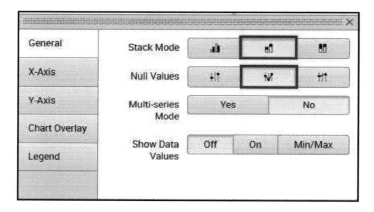

3. Click on **Apply**. The panel will change right away.
4. Remove the _time label as it is already implied. You can do this in the **X-Axis** section by setting the **Title** to **None**. Close the **Format Visualization** window by clicking on the **X** in the upper-right corner:

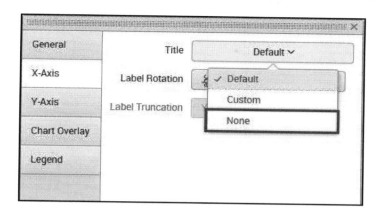

Here is the new stacked area chart panel:

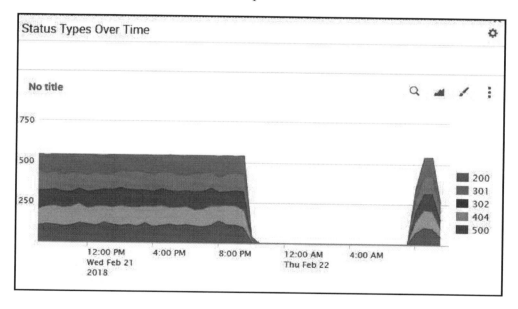

Column with overlay combination chart – Hits vs Response Time

When representing two or more kinds of data with different ranges, using a combination chart—in this case combining a column and a line—can tell a bigger story than one metric and scale alone. We'll use the **Hits vs Response Time** panel to explore the combination charting options:

1. In the **Hits vs Response Time** panel, change the chart panel visualization to **Column**
2. In the **Visualization Options** window, click on **Chart Overlay**
3. In the **Overlay** selection box, select **response_time**
4. Turn on **View as Axis**
5. Click on **X-Axis** from the list of options on the left of the window and change the **Title** to **None**
6. Click on **Legend** from the list of options on the left
7. Change the **Legend Position** to **Bottom**
8. Click on the **X** in the upper-right-hand corner to close the **Visualization Options** window

   The new panel will now look similar to the following screenshot. From this and the prior screenshot, you can see there was clearly an outage in the overnight hours:

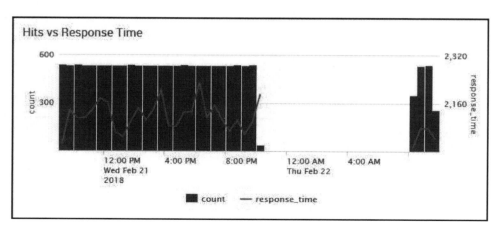

9. Click on **Done** to save all the changes you made and exit the **Edit** mode

The dashboard has now come to life. This is how it should look now:

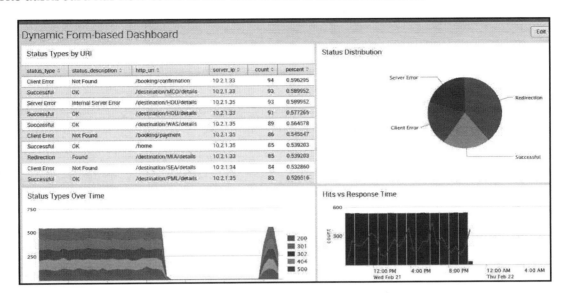

Dynamic form-based dashboard with four panels in different formats

Form inputs

With the dashboard layout complete, it is time to make it dynamic and interactive. Before jumping into the exercises, however, we'll review the key concepts related to form inputs first.

Just as in any web page, a form input is an element that allows you to select or type in information that will be submitted to the application for processing. There are different form inputs available for Splunk dashboards:

- **Text** (key in free-form text)
- **Radio** (uses a radio button convention)
- **Dropdown** (uses a menu or list to select a single option)
- **Checkbox**
- **Multiselect** (similar to **Dropdown**, allowing you to select multiple choices)
- **Link** list (this is a horizontal list that contains clickable links)
- **Time**

In this list is also the **Submit** option. This is an action button. If you decide not to autorun the dashboard on change of input selection, the **Submit** button will execute the dashboard with updated selections when clicked.

It's important the inputs you build are relevant and clear to the user, and selections may be description fields found in Lookup tables as opposed to the event itself.

 Tip from the Fez: Don't forget about performance. Rerunning the dashboard needs to be quick, otherwise the flexibility of changing inputs on the fly is marginalized. Target under 10 seconds at initial benchmark, but consider under 5 seconds for critical users and insights.

Going back into **Edit** mode for your dashboard, you will see this list of options by clicking on the **Add Input** drop-down menu:

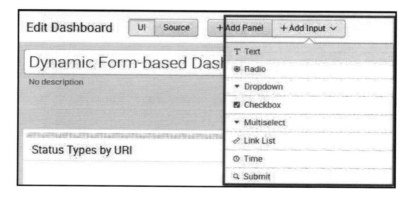

1. Select **Text** in the **Add Input** drop-down. A new editable input field panel will be added at the very top of the dashboard. You can either edit the properties of the field using the pencil icon or delete the field entirely using the **X** icon:

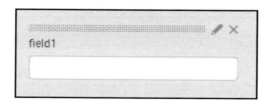

2. Click on the pencil icon to edit the properties. You can change the type of input by clicking on the selections on the left of the pop up window:

Although the options are generally different for every type of input, there are common concepts that you need to fully comprehend. So, it is worth looking at this list carefully before we take you through some examples.

In the **General** section, you'll see the following options:

- **Label**: Every input needs a label. This is a free form message shown to the user on the dashboard to indicate what the user should do, for example, `Select a Date Range:` or `Select Response Code:`.
- **Search on Change**: If checked, this checkbox triggers a reload of the dashboard panels that depend on the specific input. Ensure that you know the requirements of your users to know whether this feature should be enabled.

In the **Token Options** section, you'll see the following option:

- **Token**: This is what is used to associate the value from the form input to the search itself. In programming, this is what you would refer to as a variable. For example, if you created an input for time and you named the token `time1`, then in your panel's search query you can extract the value of the input field by calling the identifier, `$time1$`. Then, the tokens that we use to get specific fields will be `$time1$.earliest` and `$time1$.latest`. You will walk through examples of this in this chapter.

- **Default**: On inputs that require a selection, you can specify a default value during page load. This is important if your panel charts require an initial value to populate the data. If not, your panels will not load data until the user selects an option.
- Explore the messages next to **Initial Value**, **Token Prefix**, and **Token Suffix** in the UI by hovering the pointer over the question mark next to each item to understand their functions.

If you're still in the options for the **Text** input, change it to **Radio**. This will expose two more sections: **Static Options** and **Dynamic Options**. In **Static Options**, you will see the following:

- **Name and Value**: These are name-value pairs that will appear in the selection of the input field, thereby creating a manual list of value options

In the **Dynamic Options** section, you'll see the following options:

- **Search String**: Occasionally, the selection that you need shown in the input fields is already in Splunk, either in the event or in a Lookup. With this option, you can use a search query to populate the input field dynamically. For example, the search query `index=main | top host` will allow the input field to show the top hosts as the possible options to select.
- **Time Range**: This is the time range for the search query used previously. Try to use a small time range here.
- **Field for Label**: This is the field that returns the value you need, based on the search string. In the previous example, you need the **host** field.
- **Field for Value**: You can change the field for the value, but we recommend you use the same one as the label. The value is what is actually applied to the search.

Creating a time range input

Let's change our input field into a time range field:

1. On the list to the left for the first input, select **Time**.
2. In the **General** section, type **Select Time Range** in the **Label** space.
3. Click on the **Search on Change** checkbox.
4. Enter **time** for the **Token** value.
5. Set the **Default** time range to **Last 24 hours**.

6. Click **Apply** when done.

7. Use the following screenshot as a guide:

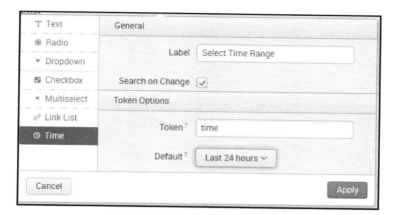

8. Before you save the dashboard changes, click the **Autorun dashboard** checkbox, as seen in the following screenshot. Then click on **Save**:

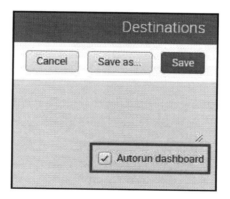

You can now try to change the time range using the time input, but nothing will happen. This is because we have not yet configured the panels to react when the time input has been changed. In these next steps, we are adjusting the searches to consider the token filled by the input selection. Let us do that now:

1. Go back to **Edit** to allow for dashboard changes

2. Select the **Edit Search** (magnifying glass) icon

3. Change **Time Range** to **Shared Time Picker (time)**

4. Click on **Apply**:

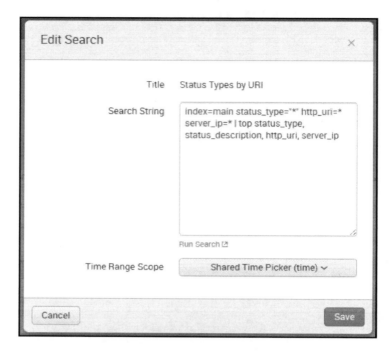

5. Click on **Save** to exit Dashboard Edit mode

At this point, the first dashboard panel should react to the changes made to the time range input. If the changes to the input aren't being recognized by search, refresh the browser to make sure you are using the freshest dashboard code. During testing for this book, we stumbled across this challenge.

Update the remaining three panels by performing the same steps. Ensure each panel changes based on your selected time range before moving on to the next section.

Creating a radio input

Now, we are going to create radio inputs with dynamic searches used to drive the input value choices. This will allow users to select server and status types, and will affect the information rendered by the panels:

1. Click on **Edit**.
2. Select **Add Input | Radio**.
3. Click on the **Edit** icon in the newly created input.
4. In the **Label** field, type in Select Server:.
5. Enable **Search on Change** by checking the checkbox.
6. In the **Token** field, type server:

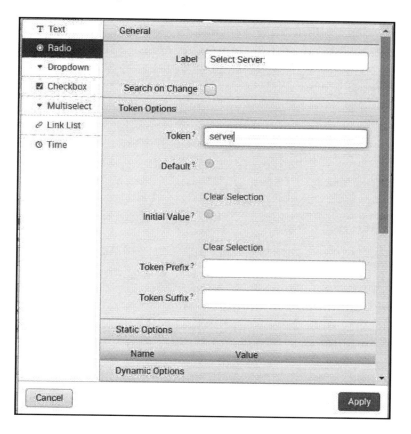

7. Scroll down to **Static Options** and click on it. In **Static Options**, add **Name** as ALL and **Value** as *.

8. Click on **Dynamic Options**, then fill in **Search String**, entering the following search command:

```
SPL> index=main | top server_ip
```

9. Update the time range to **Last 60 minutes**.

10. In **Field For Label**, type in server_ip.

11. In **Field For Value**, type in server_ip:

12. Now, scroll back up to **Token Options**.
13. For **Default**, select **ALL**.
14. For **Initial Value**, select **ALL**.
15. Click on **Apply** and you're done:

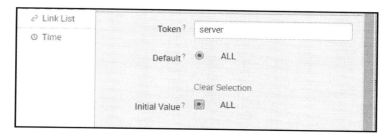

Now that you have configured the radio input with dynamic search options, you will see that the selection has been populated, along with the static option that you created. This is a great way of creating selection inputs when you know that the items will regularly change, depending on a search query:

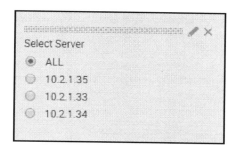

Try this exercise to reinforce what you have learned. Create a second radio input option, following the same steps as previously, with the following information:

- **Label: Select Status Type:**
- **Search on Change:** Check
- **Token:** status_type
- **Static Options: (Name: ALL, Value: *)**
- **Search String:** index=main | top status_type
- **Time Range: Last 60 minutes**
- **Field For Label:** status_type

- **Field For Value**: `status_type`
- **Token Options Default**: **ALL**
- **Token Options Initial Value**: **ALL**

Click on **Apply** to save your changes.

If you did it correctly, the newly created radio input will look similar to this:

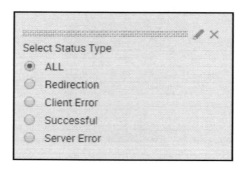

Similar to when we first created the **Time** input, the panels will not react to these new inputs until we associate them. In order for the new inputs to change the values in the panels, we have to modify each panel search string to include the new tokens, `server` and `status_type`:

1. For the **Status Types by URI** panel, click on the **Edit Search** icon.
2. Carefully update the `Search string`, adding the highlighted changes, which are as follows. This will filter the search results to show information for the selected `status_type` and `server_ip`:

   ```
   SPL> index=main status_type=$status_type$ server_ip=$server$
             | top status_type, status_description, http_uri,
        server_ip
   ```

3. Click on **Apply** to save the changes to the form input.
4. Click on **Done** to exit out of **Edit** mode.
5. Refresh the entire page using your browser's refresh icon.
6. Now, change the selections of both the **Select Server** input and the **Select Status Type** input, and make sure that the data on the first panel is changing. If it is not, ensure you refresh your browser.

Here is an example of data being filtered to **10.2.1.34** and **Redirection** for data arriving in the **Last 60 minutes**:

Select Time Range:		Select Server:		Select Status Type:	
Last 15 minutes ∨		○ ALL		○ ALL	
		○ 10.2.1.35		◉ Redirection	
		○ 10.2.1.33		○ Client Error	
		◉ 10.2.1.34		○ Server Error	
				○ Successful	

Status Types by URI

status_type ⇕	status_description ⇕	http_uri ⇕	server_ip ⇕	count ⇕	percent ⇕
Redirection	Moved Permanently	/auth	10.2.1.34	5	11.904762
Redirection	Moved Permanently	/destination/WAS/details	10.2.1.34	4	9.523810
Redirection	Found	/home	10.2.1.34	3	7.142857
Redirection	Moved Permanently	/destination/PML/details	10.2.1.34	2	4.761905
Redirection	Moved Permanently	/destination/MIA/details	10.2.1.34	2	4.761905
Redirection	Moved Permanently	/destination/MCO/details	10.2.1.34	2	4.761905
Redirection	Moved Permanently	/destination/HOU/details	10.2.1.34	2	4.761905
Redirection	Moved Permanently	/booking/reservation	10.2.1.34	2	4.761905
Redirection	Moved Permanently	/booking/payment	10.2.1.34	2	4.761905
Redirection	Found	/destination/PML/details	10.2.1.34	2	4.761905

At this point, you will appreciate what form input does to your dashboard. By simply introducing tokens in your search string, you are dynamically altering the panel charts so your users can filter the data in the ways they need, which allows them to answer many different questions with the same dashboard output. Continue editing the remaining panels using the following guide. Refresh your browser if the changes do not happen right away:

1. Edit the **Status Distribution** panel to show the top 10 status types:

   ```
   SPL> index=main status_type=$status_type$
        http_uri=* server_ip=$server$ | top status_type
   ```

2. Edit the **Status Types Over Time** panel to show a timechart with counts reflecting status code and server input selections:

   ```
   SPL> index=main status_type=$status_type$
        http_uri=* server_ip=$server$ | timechart count by
   http_status_code
   ```

3. Edit the **Hits vs Response Time** accordingly:

```
SPL> index=main status_type=$status_type$
     http_uri=* server_ip=$server$ | timechart count,
     avg(http_response_time) as response_time
```

Creating a drop-down input

Drop-down inputs function exactly the same as radio inputs. The former is used when the selection is huge and you do not want the list of choices to unnecessarily clutter the entire page. The http_uri field has numerous results, so this makes a dropdown the ideal candidate for input here.

Follow the same procedure as for radio input creation, but make sure you have selected **Dropdown** instead. Use the following information and screenshots as guides to complete the task:

1. Click on **Edit**
2. Select **Add Input | Dropdown**
3. Click the **Edit** icon for the newly created input
4. In the **Label** field, type in Select HTTP URI: to name your new dropdown
5. As you did when you created a radio button, enable **Search on Change** by checking the checkbox
6. In the **Token** field, type http_uri
7. For **Static Options**, type (Name: ALL, Value: *)
8. Under **Token Options** section, in **Default**, select ALL
9. Under **Token Options** section, in **Initial Value**, select ALL
10. Under **Dynamic Options**, be sure the search icon is selected
11. In the search string, type the following to designate that you want the index labeled main and top zero to designate that you want to return all values of http_uri:

    ```
    SPL> index=main | top 0 http_uri
    ```

12. For the time range, specify **Last 60 minutes**
13. In **Field for Label**, type http_uri
14. In the **Field for Value**, also enter http_uri
15. Click on **Apply** to save your changes:

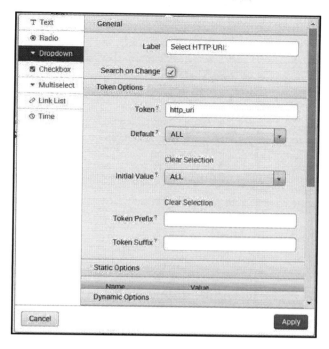

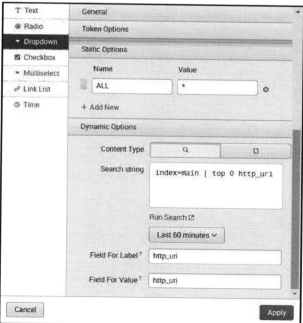

If done correctly, the newly created drop-down input will look like this:

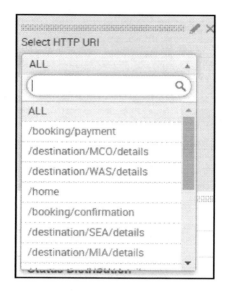

Now that you have created the drop-down input, go ahead and associate its token with the search panels. The same procedure applies; you have to edit each search string to include the new token:

1. Add the new **Dropdown** token you have created to the **Status Types by URI** panel, which will return the top 10 (by default) status types, along with their status descriptions, http_uri values, and server_ip values: http_uri=$http_uri$:

   ```
   SPL> index=main status_type=$status_type$ http_uri=$http_uri$
        server_ip=$server$ | top status_type, status_description,
        http_uri, server_ip
   ```

2. Also add the same token to the **Status Types Over Time** panel, which will then return a timechart of the top 10 counts for http_status_code:

   ```
   SPL> index=main status_type=$status_type$ http_uri=$http_uri$
        server_ip=$server$ | timechart count by http_status_code
   ```

3. And finally, add the token to the **Hits vs Response Time** panel, which will return a timechart showing the top 10 counts and average values of `http_response_time` (labeled as `response_time`):

```
SPL> index=main status_type=$status_type$ http_uri=$http_uri$
    server_ip=$server$ | timechart count, avg(http_response_time)
as
    response_time
```

When all the form inputs are done, this is how it should look. We first show the heading, where you can filter:

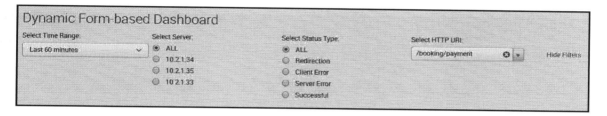

This is now a fully functional, dynamic, form-based dashboard:

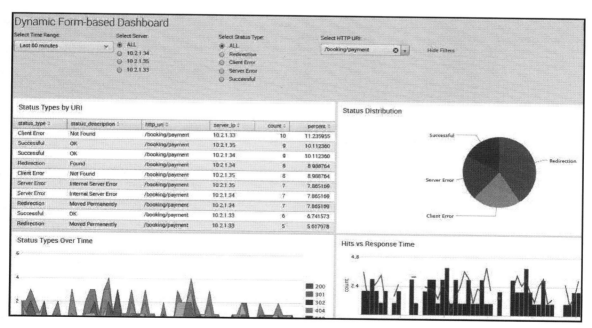

Dynamic form-based dashboard with four chart panels

Static real-time dashboard

In this section, we will create a real-time dashboard that will display crucial information based on the data we have. To encourage you, we present a screenshot here and show how it will look when we are done:

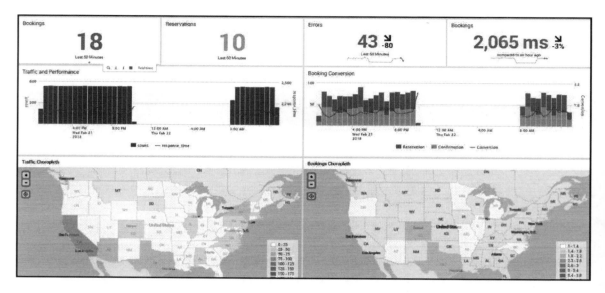

Test real-time dashboard with advanced indicators, combo charts, and choropleth charts

Single-value panels with color ranges

In the previous sections, you first created panels by running searches and then saving them as dashboard panels. You then started to modify the visualization in each panel. This is one way to build a dashboard. However, you may first want to see the visualization before adding it to a dashboard. We will use that method in this real-time dashboard exercise:

1. Let's start with a search command in the **Destinations** app to begin creating the dashboard:

```
SPL> index=main http_uri=/booking/confirmation http_status_code=200
     | stats count
```

2. Select **Real-Time | 1 hour window** in the **Time Range** preset and run the search.
3. Click on the **Visualization** tab to switch to visualization mode:

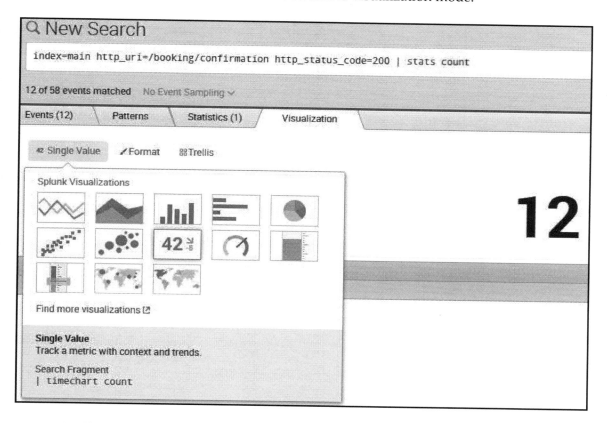

4. Click on the **Format** dropdown.

5. In the **Caption** field, type `Last 60 Minutes:`

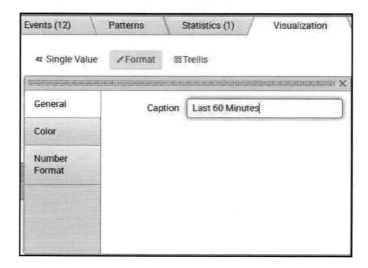

6. In the **Color** tab, click on **Yes** to **Use Colors**.
7. Arrange the color ranges to match the following screenshot:

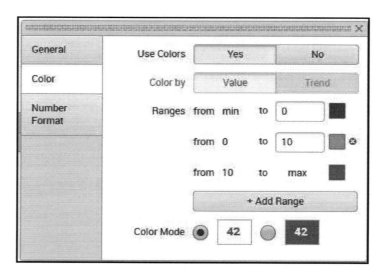

8. Changes are automatically applied. Close the **Format Visualization** window by clicking on the **X** in the upper-right corner.
9. Click on **Save As | Dashboard** panel.
10. Select **New dashboard** and fill in the following information:

11. Click on **Save**.
12. Click on **View Dashboard**.

The panel you just created is set to **Real Time search** and will continuously update as long as the page is in view and you have not exceeded your real-time search quota.

Creating panels by cloning

There will be times when you will need the same visualization for a different set of data. A very quick way of doing this is by cloning previously created panels. We will create another color-coded single value panel by cloning the one we just created:

1. In your **Real Time** dashboard, go to edit mode by clicking on the **Edit** button.
2. Click on **Add Panel**. The **Add Panel** slide-through will appear.
3. Expand **Clone from Dashboard**.
4. Expand **Real Time Dashboard**.
5. Click on **Bookings**. Use the following screenshot as a guide:

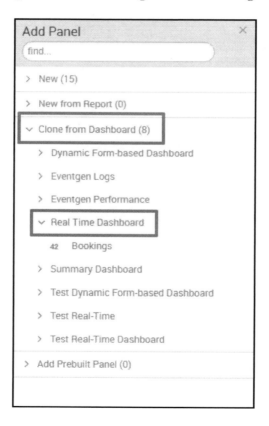

6. In the **Preview** pane, click on **Add to Dashboard**.
7. Click on the label of the second **Bookings** panel and rename it `Reservations`.
8. Then click on the **Edit Search** icon.
9. Change the **Search String** to the following command:

```
SPL> index=main http_uri=/booking/reservation http_status_code=200
| stats count
```

10. Click on **Apply**.
11. Drag the second panel to the right of the first panel so they are in the same row.
12. Click on **Save** to save your settings.

You have successfully cloned a panel and shortened its creation by a number of steps.

Single-value panels with trends

We will now create two more single-value panels that indicate trend lines. This is useful when you need your viewer to understand the behavior of the data in a very compressed line chart while highlighting the most current value:

1. Enter dashboard edit mode by clicking on the **Edit** button.
2. Create a clone of the **Bookings** panel. Follow the steps in the previous section.
3. Add it to the dashboard.
4. Rename the new panel **Errors**.
5. Change the **Search String** to the following command:

```
SPL> index=main http_status_code=5* | timechart count
```

6. Click on **Apply**.
7. Click on the **Format Visualization** icon.
8. In the **Compared to** dropdown, select **1 hour before**.
9. Ensure that **Show Sparkline** is set to **Yes**.

10. Refer to the following screenshot:

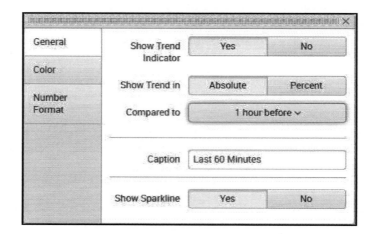

11. Click on the **X** to close the **Format Visualization** window.
12. Click on the **Search** dropdown | **Edit Search String**.
13. In the second Time Range selection, change from **1 hour window** by clicking on it. Then, click on **Real-time**.
14. Change the **Earliest** value to **24 Hours Ago**:

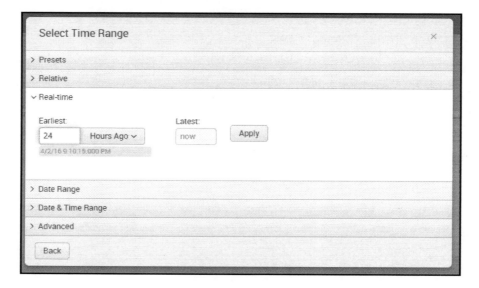

15. Click on **Apply**, and then on **Apply** again to close the **Edit Search** window.
16. Drag the panel to the right end of the first row.
17. Click on the **Save** button.

Repeat the previous procedure to create another panel. Use the following information to build the new panel and place it next to the other single-value panels in your dashboard as shown here:

- **Title**: Response Time
- **Search String**: index=main | timechart avg(http_response_time) as response_time span=1h
- **Time Range: Real-time | 24 Hours Ago**
- **Unit**: ms
- **Unit Position: After**
- **Caption**: compared to an hour ago
- **Show Trend in: Percent**

The new single-value panels have been created and are packed with information. First you see the current value within the last hour, then you see an upward or downward trend, and finally you see a sparkline (or trend line) that spans 24 hours.

The first row will now look similar to the following screenshot:

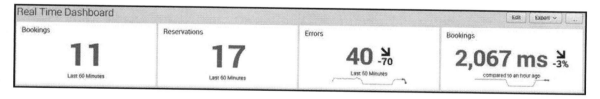

Real-time column charts with line overlays

It is time to build the second row of your real-time dashboard. Once again, we will use the cloning panel function:

1. Enter edit mode with the **Edit** button
2. Click on **Add Panel**

3. Clone the panel from the dynamic form-based dashboard **Hits vs Response Time**:

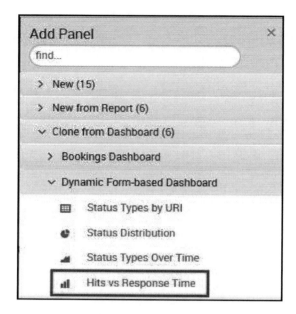

4. Click on **Add to Dashboard**

Do not be surprised if the graph is not generated. Remember we are cloning from a form-based dashboard with input tokens.

5. Rename the panel to `Traffic and Performance`
6. Change the search string to remove input token references:

```
SPL> index=main | timechart count, avg(http_response_time) as
response_time
```

7. Change the **Time Range Scope** to **Used time picker**
8. Change the **Time Range** to **Real-time** and set its value as **24 Hours Ago**
9. Click on **Apply twice** to save changes to the search and return to editing the dashboard
10. The chart will now populate the data
11. Click on **Save**

We will create another panel similar to the one we made previously. But this time, we will clone from the previous one to make our task easier:

1. Reload the browser. This is needed to load the newly-created panels in the clone selections.
2. Enter edit mode via the **Edit** button.
3. Clone the **Hits vs Response Time** panel by selecting it and adding it to the dashboard:

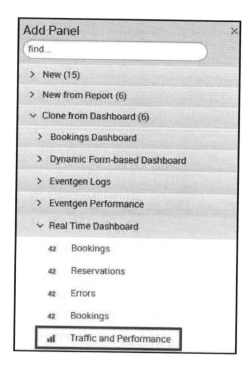

4. Rename the new panel to **Booking Conversion**.
5. Change the **Search String**:

```
SPL> index=main http_uri=/booking/reservation OR
        http_uri=/booking/confirmation
        | timechart count by http_uri | rename
/booking/confirmation AS
        Confirmation, /booking/reservation AS Reservation
        | eval Conversion=Reservation/Confirmation
        | fields _time, Reservation, Confirmation, Conversion
```

6. Ensure the **Time Range** of **Real-time | 24 Hours Ago** is still enabled from the clone process.
7. Click on **Apply**.
8. Click on the **Format Visualization** icon.
9. Select the second option in **Stack Mode** as `stacked`.
10. Click **Chart Overlay**.
11. Delete the `response_time` overlay.
12. Add the **Conversion** overlay.
13. Turn on **View** as **Axis**.
14. Click on the **X** to close the **Format Visualization** window.
15. Drag this panel to the right of the second row.

You have completed the real-time version of the combo charts. It should look similar to the following screenshot:

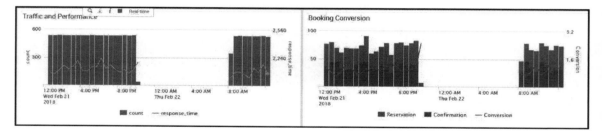

Real-time combo charts with line overlays

Creating a choropleth map

A choropleth map, whose name comes from two Greek words meaning area/region and multitude, is a two-dimensional map where areas are designated by color shades or patterns to indicate the measured strength of a statistical indicator, such as sales per area or crime rates.

We will not cover in detail the mathematical details of how a choropleth is created, but we are fortunate that we can use Splunk to provide this effective visualization tool for us. We will create two choropleth maps to denote bookings by region and traffic by region.

Since we don't have a panel to clone from, we will create this from scratch:

1. Enter edit mode with the **Edit** button.
2. Click on **Add Panel**.
3. Select **New | Choropleth Map**.
4. **Change Time Range** to a **1 hour window** under the real-time presents.
5. In **Content Title**, type in `Traffic Choropleth`.
6. Type in this **Search String**, which includes a `geomap` command and makes use of one of the two geographic lookup maps that are included by default with Splunk. The one used here includes the United States; the other one is for the world. This `geomap` command asks for a map with the counts for different states. Shading is based on the relative magnitudes of the counts:

   ```
   SPL> index=main | iplocation client_ip | stats count by Region
        | rename Region as featureId | geom geo_us_states
   ```

7. Click on **Add to Dashboard**.
8. Click the **Format Visualization** icon in the panel just created.
9. We will now put the United States in the center of the map and adjust the zoom level.
10. Change **Latitude** to 39.
11. Change **Longitude** to -98.
12. Change **Zoom** to 4:

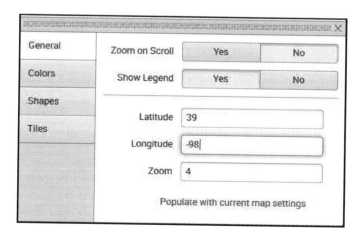

13. Click on the **Colors** tab.
14. **Change Number of Bins** to 9. This will increase the color range by adding more gradient tones:

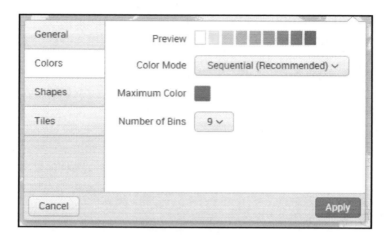

15. Click on the **X** to close the window.
16. Click on **Save**.

Now, reload your browser to allow this new panel to be added to the cloning panel selection.

Clone the **Traffic Choropleth** panel and change two things:

- **Title**: Bookings Choropleth
- **Search String**: index=main http_uri=/booking/confirmation http_status_code=200 | iplocation client_ip | stats count by Region | rename Region as featureId | geom geo_us_states

Now, drag and position the second choropleth panel to the right of the other one to make the dashboard fluid.

You have now created a real-time, multi-panel dashboard. When you use this with your real production data, you can create a visualization that is useful and can produce all kinds of efficiencies. Your hard work can become a big hit!

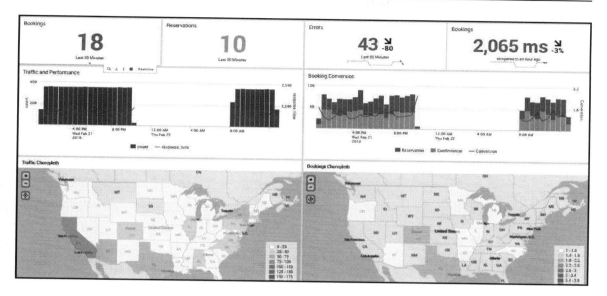

Dashboard with advanced indicators, combo charts with line overlays, and choropleth charts

Summary

In this chapter, you delved deeper into dashboard creation. You learned about the different types of dashboards and how to create them. You created a fully functional form-based dashboard that allowed you to change the inputs and affect the dashboard data, by using tokens and assigning them to search panels. Through this process, you also created and modified advanced visualization options. Finally, you learned how to create a real-time dashboard with advanced visualization panels such as Single Value with Trends and choropleth maps.

6
Data Models and Pivot

In larger organizations, not every user wants to or should have to write a Splunk search to get analytical values. Many users will want to create their owns reports and analyses in an ad hoc fashion, but will reject tools that force them to write what they perceive as code.

Splunk data models and the Pivot tool work hand in hand to meet the needs of these types of people. These functionalities enable more casual end users to generate statistical data and charts without needing to know **Search Processing Language (SPL)**.

A data model is a hierarchical mapping of data based on search results. The output of the data model's underlying search queries can be visualized as a set of rows and columns in a spreadsheet, using the Pivot tool.

The Pivot tool is what is used to present data fields as rows and columns of data. Using the Pivot tool, a user can create a crosstab report or a visualization, for example. Users can also apply additional ad hoc filtering and set up choices with pointing and clicking, rather than typing.

In this chapter, we will learn how to:

- Create a data model
- Enable acceleration for the data model
- Create a Pivot output
- Visualize data using the area chart, pie chart, and single value with trend sparkline options

Creating a data model

To create a data model of our existing Eventgen data, perform the following steps:

1. In the **Destinations** app, click on the **Settings** menu. Under the **Knowledge Objects** section, select **Data Models**. This page will be empty until you have created your first data model.

2. Click on the **New Data Model** button in the upper-right corner of the screen to proceed.

3. In the **Data Models** screen, click on **New Data Model**.

4. Give your new data model a **Title** and **ID**, and ensure that it is created in the **Destinations** app. Refer to the following screenshot as a guide:

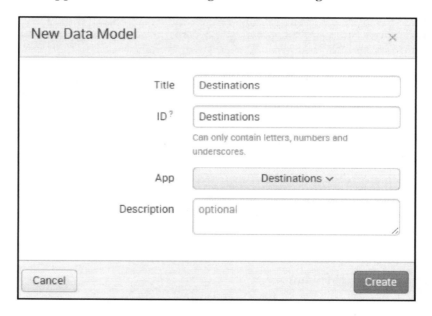

5. Click on **Create**. You are now in the Destinations data model editing page.
6. Click on the **Add Dataset** dropdown and select **Root Event**. The concept of data model hierarchy is now in play. The **Root Event** or **Root Search** is the base search that will populate the data for the entire data model tree.
7. Populate the **Root Event** with the fields seen in the following screenshot. We want to create a data model for our Eventgen data, so we use `index=main` as the primary constraint:

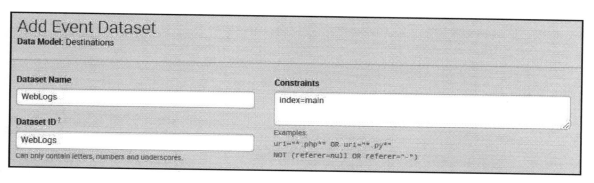

8. Click on the **Preview** button to ensure that the `index=main` search returns the expected results.
9. Click on **Save**.

After saving the root event, additional attributes will be created as default. Because data models respect hierarchies, these initial attributes will be inherited by all child objects. Attributes or fields that are generic to all data regardless of search constraints need to be created in the root object.

Adding attributes to objects

There are different ways to add an attribute to an object. In this book, we will utilize extracted attributes based on fields and regular expressions. Go ahead and carry out these steps:

1. Click on the **Add Field** dropdown and select **Auto-Extracted**.
2. Scroll down the list of auto-extracted fields and select the fields that we have manually extracted in Chapter 2, *Bringing in Data*, as listed and shown in the bullet list, followed by the screenshot:
   - http_method
   - http_response_time
   - http_status_code
   - http_uri
   - http_user_agent

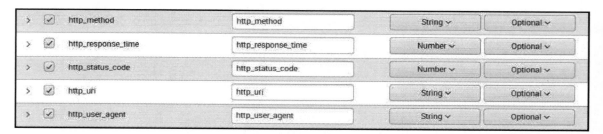

3. If you look closely, you'll see Splunk has automatically classified the attributes based on assumed data type (for instance **String** for http_method and **Number** for http_status_code). You can do the same steps if you missed an attribute.

Your newly added attributes are now in the **Extracted** section and will also be inherited by all child objects, as a child object in Splunk inherits the constraints and attributes of a parent object.

 Tip from the Fez: You've just seen how work completed in an earlier chapter is reused, in this case, fields extracted from our data source. As your Splunk environment grows, a constant push to consolidate and standardize logic and fields will improve data quality, as well as Splunk's general usability for casual and business users.

Creating child objects

To create a child object, do the following:

1. Select the **WebLogs** event, click on the **Add Dataset** dropdown, and select **Child**
2. Populate the form with the following information:
   - **Dataset Name**: Authenticated
   - **Additional Constraints**: http_uri="/auth"
3. Click on **Preview** to review
4. Click on **Save** to proceed
5. Click on the **Authenticated** child object (under **WebLogs** in the upper left) and observe that all the attributes of the root object have been inherited

Create more child objects of the root object, **WebLogs**:

Object name	Additional constraints
Booking Confirmation	http_uri="/booking/confirmation"
Booking Payment	http_uri="/booking/payment"
Destination Details	http_uri="/destination/*/details"
Destinations Search	http_uri="/destinations/search"

You now have five child objects that are differentiated by the pages viewed in your web log as shown in the following screenshot:

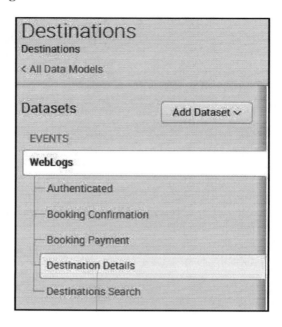

Tip from the Fez: It's important to know the analytical requirements of the data in question to ensure that you create the right starting points for users, whether that is the root event or child objects.

Creating an attribute based on a regular expression

Now, we are going to create an attribute based on a regular expression, which is a specialized text string that describes a search pattern. What we want to do is extract the airport code that is part of the **Destination Details** URI:

```
http_uri="/destination/MIA/details"
```

To do this, we have to create an attribute in the **Destination Details** child. Follow these steps:

1. Select **Destination Details**, click on the **Add Field** dropdown, and select **Regular Expression**.
2. In the **Regular Expression** field, type in the following text:

   ```
   /destination/(?<AirportCode>.+?)/details
   ```

3. Click on the blank area outside the text box to populate the field, as shown in the following screenshot.
4. Change the display name to `Airport Code:`

Regular Expression

5. Click on **Preview** and make sure that the airport codes are highlighted in the events. You can also click the **Airport Code** tab to see them summarized:

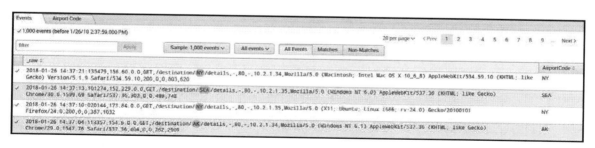

Airport Code tab

6. Click the **Non-Matches** button and ensure that no events are shown.
7. Click on **Save** to proceed.

Now that you have built your first data model, it is time to prepare it for use in Pivot. Here are the steps to perform:

1. Change the permission of the data model so that all other Splunk users can use it in the context of the **Destinations** app. On the **Edit** dropdown, select **Edit Permissions**:

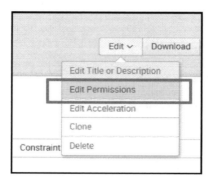

2. Change the permission of the data model so that it is available for the **Destinations** app. Click on **App** on the **Display For** button set.
3. Set the **Read** permission to **Everyone** and the **admin** group to **Write**:

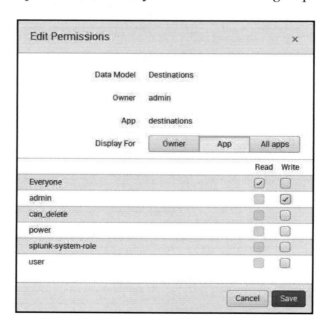

4. Click on **Save** to continue. In the next section, we will introduce you to data model acceleration and how to enable it.

Data model acceleration

When you enable acceleration for a data model, Splunk internally pre-summarizes the data defined by the data model for a given time range. This gives a tremendous boost to the search speed for your data model when searches are executed within the given time range. There are a couple of things to remember when you enable data model acceleration:

1. Once you enable acceleration for a data model, you will no longer be able to edit the data model objects. Ensure that your model and related child objects and attributes are accurate before implementing acceleration. A huge data model may take some time to complete the acceleration process, so plan accordingly. You will only be able to edit the data model again if you disable the acceleration.

2. Select your summary range wisely. The summary range is the calculation time span that the acceleration will use against your data. The summary range can span 1 day, 7 days, 1 month, 3 months, 1 year, and so on. Search acceleration is based on time ranges. Only those that fall within the selected time range will be accelerated. If you need to accelerate for 5 days, then it is safe to select 7 days. However, if you run the report for 10 days, the searches beyond the selected acceleration range will execute at a normal speed, which isn't always a bad thing.

3. Acceleration will take up disk space. Test sizing prior to setting the acceleration for good.

In this exercise, you will enable data model acceleration with a summary range of 7 days:

1. Once again in the **Edit** dropdown, select **Edit Acceleration**:

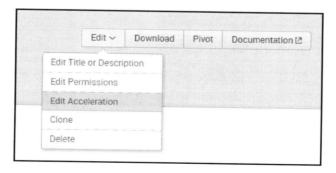

2. In the **Edit Acceleration** prompt, check the **Accelerate** box and select **7 Days** as your **Summary Range**. These options are seen in the following screenshot:

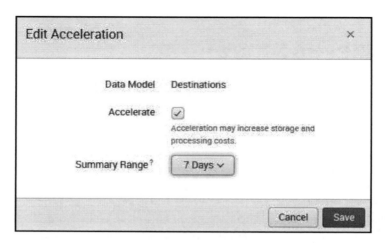

3. Click on **Save** to kick off the acceleration process. Notice that Splunk will issue a warning that the data model is locked and can no longer be edited unless you disable acceleration:

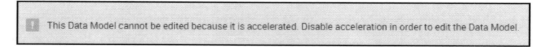

4. Let's check the status of the acceleration process. Go back to the **Data Models** main page by clicking on **All Data Models** in the upper left.

5. Expand the **Destinations** data model by clicking on the side > next to **Destinations**. You should see information that is similar to the following screenshot:

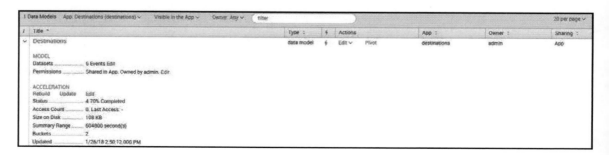

6. Under the **Acceleration** section, you will see a sizable amount of information about the state of your data model acceleration, such as the status, access count, size on disk, summary range, buckets, and the last time it got updated. It will probably take some minutes until the acceleration is complete. Keep refreshing the page until the **Status** says **100.00% Completed**, as shown in this screenshot:

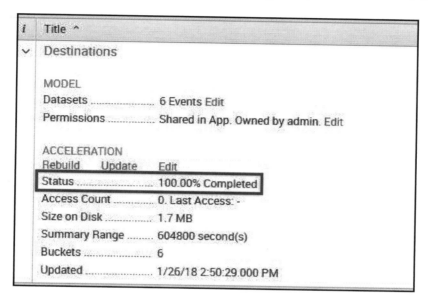

Now that the data model has been fully constructed and accelerated, it is time to use it with Pivot.

The Pivot editor

Now, we will begin to make a Pivot; follow these directions:

1. From the main data models list, click on **Pivot** in the main menu under **Actions**.

2. This time, simply click on the **WebLogs** object. You will see a page shown in the following screenshot with a count of all **WebLogs** data for **All Time**:

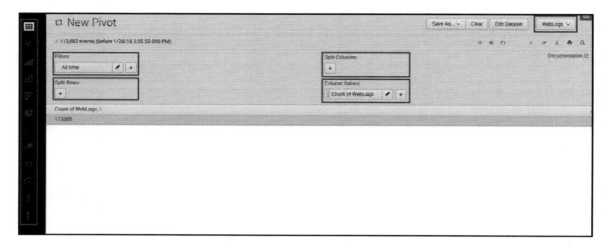

We have highlighted different sections in this page. The navigation bar icons to the left of the screen represent the different visualization modes. The default and topmost visualization is the statistics table. Generally, you will first construct your statistics table and validate data before changing to other visualizations.

The time range filtering functions the same in Pivot as it does in the Search window. Consider changing it to something within the scope of your acceleration summary range (7 days in this case) to improve performance. **Filters** will allow you to narrow down your dataset based on the data model attributes we defined earlier in this chapter.

Split Rows and **Split Columns** will allow you to change the orientation of your data based on **Time** or **Attribute**. The following screenshot shows you what attributes will appear on the **Split Columns** drop-down menu:

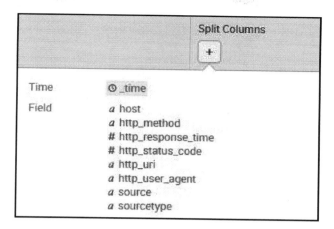

Column Values on the other hand will allow you to select an **Event** or **Attribute** based on **Time**, as shown in the following screenshot:

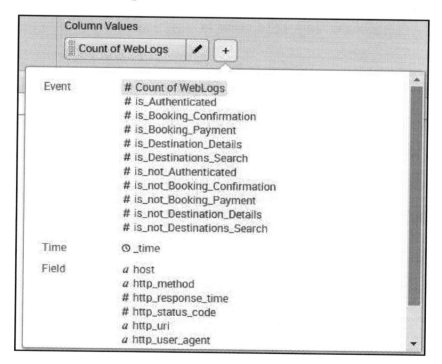

In the upper-right corner of the page, you will see the scope of the Pivot. This is usually the object that you clicked when you first entered the Pivot editor. Through this dropdown, you can switch to other data models and other objects, as shown in the following screenshot. It is also a shortcut for checking the status of acceleration:

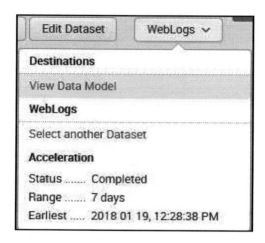

The Pivot editor will always default to the **Count** of the object that was selected in the data model. That is why, in the results section, you see **Count of WebLogs**:

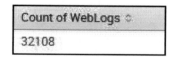

Creating a Pivot and a chart

Let's create a chart that will visualize web traffic. **WebLogs** generated by Eventgen are simulated data from a web application with varied status codes. Every line in the web log is a request from a web client (such as the browser or mobile device). In effect, the sum of all the requests and status codes equals the entire traffic of the web application.

To create a chart, do the following:

1. First, change the time range to **Last 7 days**.
2. Change **Split Rows** to _time and leave **Periods** as the default, as shown next. This is equivalent to using the `timechart` function in SPL without specifying a *span*. Leave the default sorting value as well:

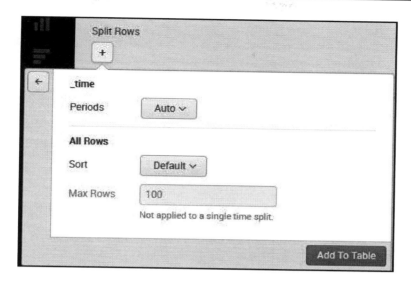

3. Click **Add To Table**. The results will change to show seven rows, with the sum of the **WebLogs** for each row value.

4. In **Split Columns**, select `http_status_code` to split the columns. There will be many options available to you to tweak your data set for the **Split Columns** function, but for now, leave them as they are and select **Add To Table**. The final selection of filters is shown in the following screenshot:

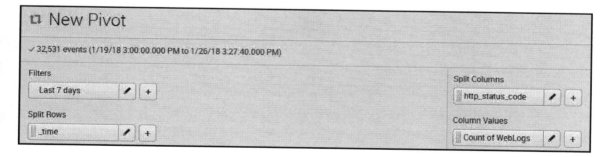

Your statistics table should have changed. The count per day has now been split based on the `http_status_code` attribute, as shown next. Since your data model is accelerated and you have selected the time filter that fits the summary range, the results should render almost instantaneously:

_time	200	301	302	404	500
2018-01-19	868	808	842	856	852
2018-01-20	666	703	663	654	689
2018-01-21	0	0	0	0	0
2018-01-22	0	0	0	0	0
2018-01-23	1093	1129	1090	1114	1127
2018-01-24	1602	1623	1601	1631	1631
2018-01-25	1953	1974	1983	2024	2062
2018-01-26	259	264	263	241	266

Creating an area chart

With the statistics Pivot complete, let's visualize the data:

1. Select the **Area Chart** visualization tool in the left menu bar, as shown in the following screenshot:

The next page will show you an array of options that you can choose from to change the way your area chart behaves, side by side with the chart. Depending on how long you have been running Splunk on your machine, you should see a stacked area chart similar to the following screenshot:

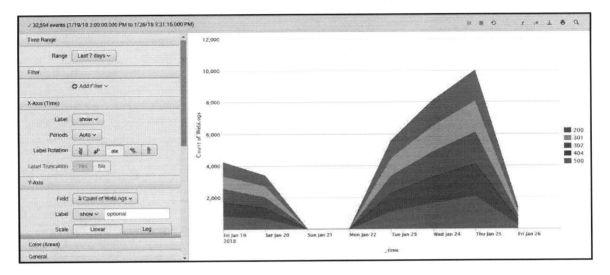

2. Here are some additional steps to improve the chart. In the **X-Axis (Time)** section, choose to **hide** the **Label**. This will remove the **_time** label on the *x* axis:

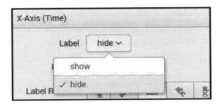

3. Scroll down in the chart settings area to the **Color (Areas)** section, and move the **Legend Position** to the bottom, as shown in this screenshot:

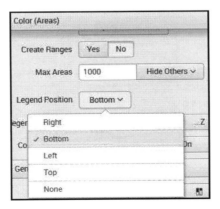

4. Your area chart is now ready to be saved as a Dashboard panel. Click on the **Save As** button and select **Dashboard Panel**.

5. Let's create a new dashboard called **Summary Dashboard**.

6. Change the permission to **Shared in App**.

7. Finally, change the **Panel Title** to **Web Traffic per Day Last 7 Days**.

8. Click on **Save** to finish and click on **View Dashboard**. Use the following screenshot as a guide:

You now have a single-panel dashboard that is driven by the data model that you just created. It should look similar to what is shown here:

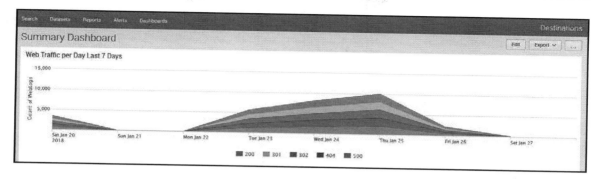

We will now add more Pivot-driven analytics to this dashboard.

Creating a pie chart

Now, let's create a pie chart to show counts of the Destinations detail logs by **Airport Code**. Recall earlier in this chapter a data model attribute was created using a regular expression to extract **Airport Code** as a field.

To create a pie chart:

1. Go back to the Pivot editor and select **Destination Details**. There are two ways to get back to the Pivot editor: either via **Settings| Data Models| Destinations**, or more easily by clicking **Datasets** in the application navigation bar. In the resulting **Datasets** listing, click on the **Explore** drop-down menu to the right of **Destination Details**:

When entering the **Datasets** via the application navigation bar for the first time, you may be prompted regarding new functionality in Splunk Enterprise, including the Splunk datasets add-on. As Splunk tells you, the datasets add-on presents search results using the visual concept of tables, akin to relational database management systems. However, the add-on is not there by default. Should this functionality be of interest, you can download and install the add-on using you Splunk account and skills you acquired in Chapter 1, *Splunk – Getting Started*.

The datasets add-on is not required for the following examples, so the new in Splunk Enterprise window can be closed.

2. Change your time range to **Last 24 hours**.
3. Select **Airport Code** from the **Split Rows** menu, and **Add to table**. Your Pivot editor should now show something similar to the following screenshot:

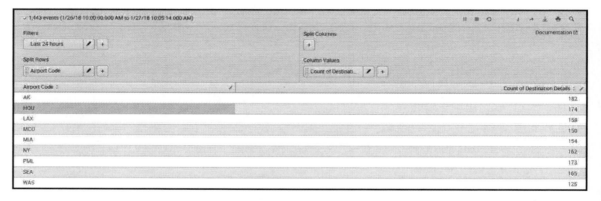

4. This data is sufficient to generate a pie chart. Go ahead and click on the **Pie Chart** icon on the navigation bar to the left:

Without additional changes, the pie chart appears. Splunk has rendered a chart subdividing the different airport codes in the last 24 hours:

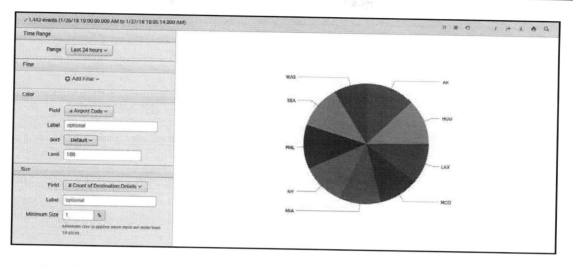

5. Add this to the **Summary Dashboard** by once again selecting **Save As** a **Dashboard panel**.

6. Click on the **Existing** button and select **Summary Dashboard**.

7. Give the panel this title: **Destinations Last 24 Hrs**.

8. Click on **Save** and go to your dashboard to see the end result:

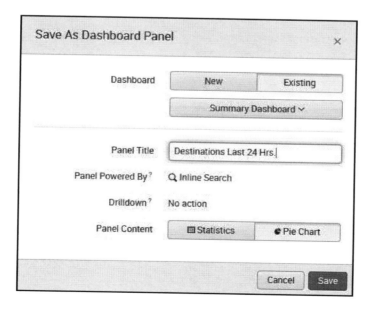

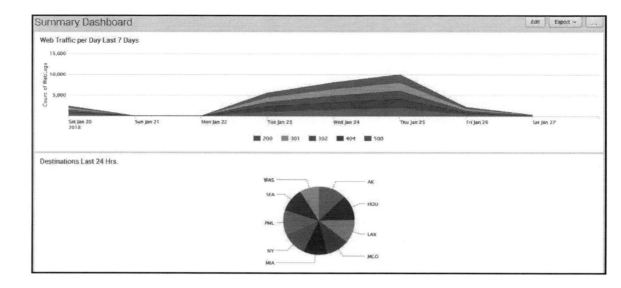

Single value with trending sparkline

We will now use one of the simpler yet powerful visualizations Splunk offers, the single value with trending sparkline:

1. Go back to the **Datasets** list and open a Pivot for **Booking Confirmation**.
2. Change your time range to **Last 24 hours**. That's all you need to do here.
3. Go ahead and click on the **Single Value** visualization option as indicated here:

4. The initial default result is a single number, but we can add context with a **Sparkline**. In the **Sparkline** section, click on **Add Sparkline**; then select **_time**. Change the **Periods** to **Hours** as shown here:

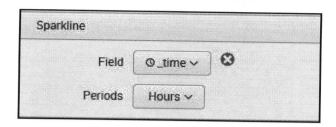

5. Splunk provides a great visualization with very few steps and no SPL. The display shows the number of **Booking Confirmations** since the start of the hour and will provide a number comparison from the hour before. It will also give you an upward or a downward arrow that depicts trends and will add a sparkline at the bottom of the number:

6. Add more context to this single number using coloring. In the **Color** section, click on **Yes** in **Use Colors**. In the **Color by** option, select **Trend**. Select the second option for **Color Mode**. Here is how the **Color** section looks now:

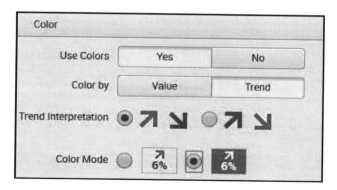

With those options selected, your visualization will now have changed to something similar to what you see next:

7. Finally, save this panel to the **Summary Dashboard** and label it as **Booking Confirmations**.

Rearranging your dashboard

To change the arrangement of the panels on the dashboard, follow these steps:

1. In the **Summary Dashboard**, click on the **Edit** button and select **Edit Panels**. This will convert the panels into widgets that you can drag around using each widgets header area.
2. Change the final layout of your **Summary Dashboard** to look like the following screenshot. Click on **Save** once you have laid the widgets out in the correct orientation:

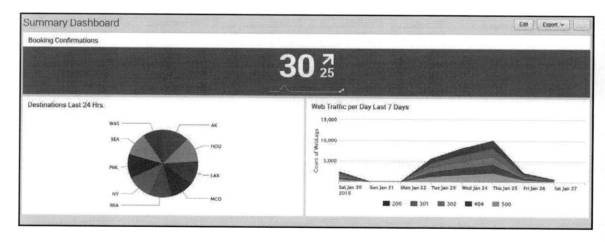

Summary Dashboard

Summary

In this chapter, we showed you how to build a three-panel dashboard without writing a single Splunk search command. Pivots can be a powerful tool to expose Splunk to business users who are data savvy, but perhaps initially resist learning to write Splunk commands to extract value from data.

To enable Pivots, we showed you how to create a data model used by the Pivot editor to create analyses, reports, and dashboards. You walked through creating your data model objects based on a hierarchy. You saw how data models can consist of attributes from existing data fields, inherited from parent objects, or extracted using a regular expression.

Finally, you used the very intuitive Pivot editor and created three different visualizations: area chart, pie chart, and single value with trend sparkline. You used those to create and organize a three-panel dashboard.

In the next Chapter 5, *Data Optimization, Reports, Alerts, and Accelerating Searches*, we will continue to explore the many other ways Splunk can provide analytical value from machine data.

HTTP Event Collector

7

In this chapter, you will learn about the Splunk **HTTP event collector (HEC)**. Metaphorically, the HEC is a catcher's mitt for Splunk to catch data sent to it via HTTP or HTTPS communication.

In this chapter, we will learn about the following topics:

- An overview of the HEC
- How data flows to the HEC
- Generating an HEC token
- Sending events in multiple formats and counts to the HEC
- Enabling and using indexer acknowledgement

What is the HEC?

The Splunk HEC is a useful and commonly used part of Splunk. The HEC does the important function of collecting and sending HTTP and HTTPS events to other systems. One common example where the HEC adds tremendous value is by capturing/sending events from/to web and mobile-based client devices. Once Splunk captures the data via the HEC from the application, it can be used for a variety of analyses related to application use and errors.

How does the HEC work?

HTTP and HTTPS events can be created and delivered by web applications containing event metadata, such as time, host, and source, as well as other event data, found in the event key. The HEC makes it easy for app developers to add a minimal amount of code to their applications to send this data to Splunk. This is all done in a secure and efficient way, making it easy for application developers to be able to Splunk their application event data.

Typically, an application generates its own log file or uses **Document Object Model** (**DOM**) tagging to generate some relevant functional metrics. This is useful and still applicable to traditional multi-page web applications. However, web page development has moved forward in recent years, with a new framework called **Single-Page Application** (**SPA**). The advancement of SPA means most of an application's work in showing HTML results happens dynamically in the client's browser. Instead of going through different HTML pages, only one HTML page is loaded when the user interacts with the app.

This advance poses a dilemma for application data monitoring. Since most of the application's interactions now occur on the client side, server-side tracking adds less value. This is where the HEC comes into its own, since a short line of JavaScript code can push event data to Splunk.

There are use cases other than web applications that may also find the HEC useful. For internal applications, the HEC can easily be utilized to keep track of events occurring in the client's UI. This is also viable for the increasingly ubiquitous **Internet of Things** (known as **IoT**, a network of devices with a variety of purposes that are hooked up to a network) for devices that can push data to other places.

How data flows to the HEC

Let's begin by looking at how data flows to the HEC. This is a multi-step process that is important to understand.

Logging data

Before Splunk can capture any data, it needs to be packaged from the source, which can be done in a number of different ways:

- A Splunk logging library for Java, JavaScript, or .NET
- Another agent, such as a JavaScript request library

- The Java Apache HTTP client
- And lastly, some other client packing data in JSON or raw formats

Before going further, let's review what the JSON format means. A couple of examples of key-value pairs in JSON format are shown here. The key is listed first, then a colon, and then the value of that key. Sequences of key-value pairs must be separated by commas:

```
{
    "time": 1519413100, // epoch time
    "host": "localhost",
    "source": "datasource",
    "sourcetype": "txt",
    "index": "main",
    "event": { "Hello world!" }
}
```

Using a token with data

In addition to the formatting of the event data, each data package will also need a token in its authorization header. The fact that the system is based on tokens means that the user doesn't have to include Splunk credentials in the application or in files that support the application, while also protecting Splunk from receiving events from unintended sources. The Splunk administrator will generate the token using Splunk and provide it to software application developers for use.

Sending out the data request

The data package, with a correct token, is then sent out as an HTTP or HTTPS request to the HEC endpoint on the instance of Splunk Enterprise.

Verifying the token

Once the HTTP/HTTPS request is captured by Splunk, the token is checked and verified against the list of known tokens. If it passes this checkpoint and is found to be a good token, then the data package is taken in by Splunk using any related configurations set in the Splunk user interface when the administrator set up the token.

Indexing the data

Once the token is verified, the data is taken by Splunk from the request and indexed. It can then be analyzed and examined using the Splunk functionality you've been learning throughout this book.

Understanding the process at a high level, let's now get started with exactly how to do this with Splunk, step by step.

We will show you specifically how Splunk can be used to improve the functioning of a web company. You will learn to do the following:

- Enable the HEC
- Create an HEC token
- Perform basic cURL statements from the command line
- Enable and use indexer acknowledgement

Enabling the HEC

First we'll enable the HEC. As we noted in the preceding section, by default, the HEC is not enabled upon initial installation of Splunk. To enable the HEC in your local Splunk instance, perform the following steps, after which you can refer to the screenshot:

1. Go to **Settings** | **Data Inputs**
2. Click on **HTTP Event Collector**
3. Click on the **Global Settings** button in the upper-right corner of the page
4. Select **Enabled** for **All Tokens**
5. Leave **Enable SSL** checked, as it should be checked by default
6. Leave the rest at the default settings so your window appears as shown here, and click on **Save**:

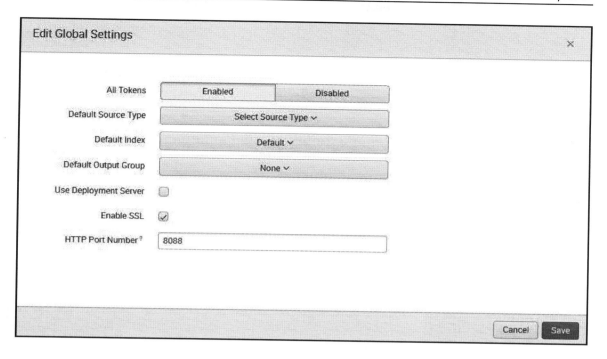

Generating an HEC authentication token

Next, you will generate an HEC authentication token. The HEC token will ensure no unknown applications have their data indexed if it arrives at your Splunk server on the assigned port. The HEC authentication token is sent in the HTTP header of the incoming request to Splunk. Without this token, the Splunk response would typically indicate a status code 401 (unauthorized error).

The HEC token will also enable you to override the source tag of all incoming data. This makes it easy to differentiate data streams later, based on where the data is coming from. It is best practice to create a separate token for each application. If something goes wrong with one application, say it starts flooding your Splunk instance with unwanted data, it will then be easy enough to disable that associated token to mitigate the issue. Follow these instructions:

1. Go to **Settings | Data Inputs**.
2. Find **HTTP Event Collector**.
3. Click on **New Token**.
4. In the **Name** field, enter Demo1.
5. Leave the other fields as it is. Note, however, that we will return to the indexer acknowledgement functionality shortly.
6. Click on **Next** to proceed:

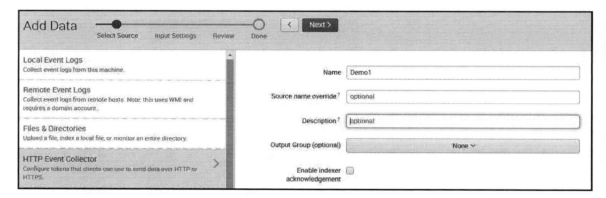

You will see an **Input Settings** page that looks like the following screenshot. Follow these instructions:

1. In the **Input Settings** page, you will create a new **Source Type**.
2. In the first **Source type** section, click on **New**.
3. Type http_events as the **Source Type**.
4. Ensure the app context is set properly to our **Destinations** app. Remember that not setting this will mean your configurations are being places in different locations from prior exercises:

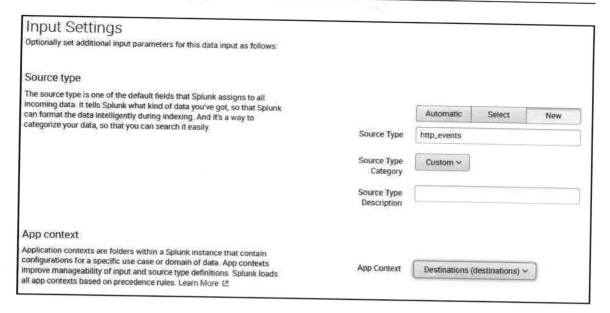

5. In the **Index** section, select **main** as the selected index.

6. **main** should also then appear in the **Default Index** setting as well:

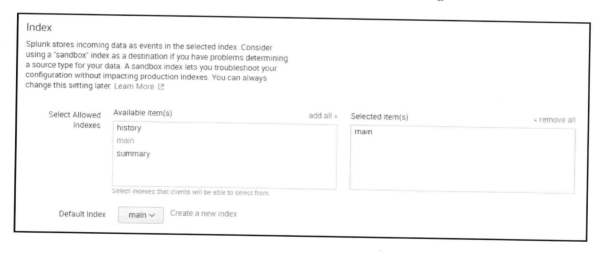

7. Click on **Review** to proceed.
8. Verify your work against the following screenshot; then click on **Submit**.

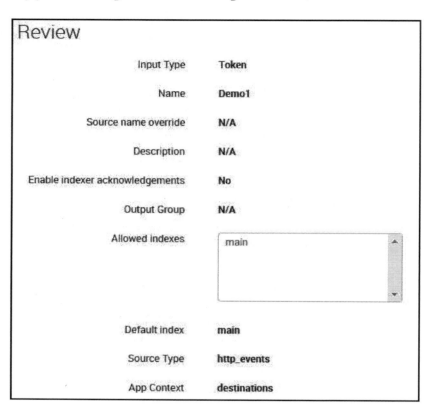

9. Once you are done, go back to **Data Inputs | HTTP Event Collector** and you should see the newly generated **Token Value**. Copy or take note of this value as you will need it for the exercises in this chapter.

The distinct token value created on your personal instance will resemble, but not be exactly the same as to, the token value shown in these screenshots. Replace the token used in these exercises with the token generated in your personal Splunk instance.

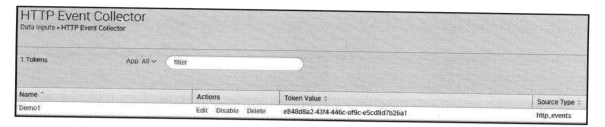

As you have learned in previous chapters, everything that you change in the Splunk UI generally makes a change to a configuration file. In this case, the new token modified the `C:\Splunk\etc\apps\destinations\local\inputs.conf` file with the relevant input content, including the token, as seen here:

```
[http://Demo1]
disabled = 0
index = main
indexes = main
sourcetype = http_events
token = e848d8a2-43f4-446c-af9c-e5cd8d7b26a1
```

Seeing the HEC in action with cURL

Now that the configuration has been quickly completed, let's see how the HEC works. We will use the **command line URL** method (**cURL**) to show the HEC in action. We will use the following information to write a cURL command:

- **URL:** `http://localhost:8088/services/collector`
- **Custom Header:** `Authorization`
- **Custom Header Value:** `Splunk <token>`
- **Content Type:** `application/json`
- **Body:** `{ "event": "Mobile Device Event - Something happened" }`

cURL is included in macOS X and most Linux distributions, such as CentOS and RHEL, and helps to transfer data to or from a server.

> For Windows users, to test the HEC using cURL, download the `curl-7.46.0-win64` file available on the book's GitHub site.

From a Linux or macOS command line, enter the following cURL command:

```
curl -k https://localhost:8088/services/collector -H 'Authorization: Splunk
e848d8a2-43f4-446c-af9c-e5cd8d7b26a1' -d '{"event":"Mobile Device Event -
Something happened"}'
```

For Windows, cURL commands require a slightly different syntax due to different behavior of single and double quotes. For Windows, what were single quotes in the Linux cURL are double quotes and double quotes are escaped out of using a backward slash.

Here is an example of the same cURL as before, except this version of the cURL is written for a Windows environment. Notice how there are back slashes prior to double quotes as Windows treats double quotes differently than Linux commands:

```
curl -k https://localhost:8088/services/collector -H "Authorization: Splunk
e848d8a2-43f4-446c-af9c-e5cd8d7b26a1" -d "{\"event\":\"Mobile Device Event
- Something happened\"}"
```

If your cURL statements are successful, you will see {"text":"Success","code":0}. You can also search from the event in the Splunk UI: index=main source=http:Demo1. There are a variety of ways to send these events, so here are some examples of additional options when sending events to the HEC, using the Linux-based syntax.

Multiple events in one HTTPS message:

```
curl -k https://localhost:8088/services/collector -H 'Authorization: Splunk
e848d8a2-43f4-446c-af9c-e5cd8d7b26a1' -d '{"event":"Mobile Device Event -
Something happened"}{"event": Mobile Device Event 2 - Something else
happened}'
```

One event with multiple fields:

```
curl -k https://localhost:8088/services/collector -H 'Authorization: Splunk
e848d8a2-43f4-446c-af9c-e5cd8d7b26a1' -d '{"event": "Mobile Device Event",
"fields": {"device": "macbook", "users": ["joe", "bob"]}}'
```

You can also use the _json sourcetype Splunk provides out of the box, as opposed to using a custom sourcetype as we have in these examples:

```
curl -k https://localhost:8088/services/collector -H 'Authorization: Splunk
e848d8a2-43f4-446c-af9c-e5cd8d7b26a1' -d '{"sourcetype": "_json", "event":
{"device": "macbook", "users": ["joe", "bob"]}}'
```

Indexer acknowledgement

Indexer acknowledgement is an additional functionality of the Splunk HEC. In the previous examples, after submitting the cURL command, Splunk would return a success message. However, such a message just confirms the event was received. It does not confirm that the event was actually indexed by Splunk. This is where the indexer acknowledgement functionality adds value.

If some or all of your HEC events are required to be captured, using HEC indexer acknowledgement will allow for checking indexing success and resending events which fail to index.

Indexer acknowledgement is configured at an HEC token level. Therefore, some tokens can include the acknowledgement functionality while others may not.

To edit the token you created in the exercises before, go to the **HTTP Event Collect** input screen:

1. Go to **Settings** | **Data Inputs**
2. Click on **HTTP Event Collector**
3. Click on the **Edit** button for your token in the **Actions** column:

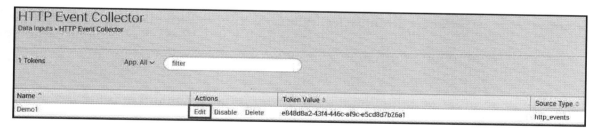

4. Check the box next to **Enable indexer acknowledgement** and then click on **Save**

Now, the original cURL statement needs to be updated to account for the acknowledgement functionality. The modified cURL is as follows, with the new updated bolded:

```
curl -k https://localhost:8088/services/collector?channel=0aeeac95-
ac74-4aa9-b30d-6c4c0ac581ba -H 'Authorization: Splunk e848d8a2-43f4-446c-
af9c-e5cd8d7b26a1' -d '{"event":"Mobile Device Event - Something
happened"}'
```

The long number after the = sign is an example of a GUID, which can be created online on sites such as `guidgenerator.com`. The specific GUID used is not important; however, it must also be used when checking the index acknowledgement status.

After submitting the preceding cURL successfully, the following message is returned:

```
{"text:"Success","code":0,"ackId":0}
```

This is a similar message as received earlier, except that now there is an additional `ackId` field returned with a numeric identifier, in this case, 0.

Submit the event another four times. Notice as you submit the events again that the `ackId` will increment for each submission. Check the acknowledgement status using the following command:

```
curl -k
https://localhost:8088/services/collector/ack?channel=0aeeac95-ac74-4aa9-b3
0d-6c4c0ac581ba -H 'Authorization: Splunk e848d8a2-43f4-446c-af9c-
e5cd8d7b26a1' -d '{"acks": [0,1,2,3,4]}'
```

Summary

In this chapter, you learned about the HEC and how it can be used to send data directly from an application to Splunk. To do this, you learned how to enable the HEC and create a token used as authorization to process the request. You also saw how to use cURL to submit event data. Lastly, you learned how to enrich the HEC functionality using index acknowledgement.

In the next chapter, we'll move on and learn more ways to work with Splunk as effectively as possible.

Best Practices and Advanced Queries

8

To build on the strong foundation of the Splunk skills attained using this book so far, we want to introduce you to a few extra skills that will help make you a powerful Splunker. Throughout the book, you have gained the essential skills required to use Splunk effectively. In this chapter, we will look at some best practices you can incorporate into your Splunk instance:

- Indexes for testing
- Searching within an index
- Searching within a limited time frame
- How to do quick searches via fast mode
- How to use event sampling
- Using the fields command to improve performance

We will also provide some advanced searches that you can use as templates when the need arises. These include:

- Doing a subsearch, or a search within a search
- Using `append` and `join`
- Using `eval` with `if`
- Using `eval` with `match`

Tip from the Fez: Throughout this book, we have seen how logs can be used to improve applications and to troubleshoot problems. Splunk comes prebuilt to recognize a large number of logging formats. However, if you need to create log files that you anticipate will be used by Splunk, consider the following recommendations Splunk provides on one of their many community and product sites: `http://dev.splunk.com/view/logging/SP-CAAAFCK`.

Indexes for testing

It is a good idea to use an index for testing purposes, especially when you need to index new data and you are not familiar with its format. You should consider creating an index just for this purpose as you are crafting solutions to load data into Splunk.

When loading data for the first time into Splunk, especially if it is a custom sourcetype, it often will not be loaded properly with all the fields recognized accurately. Performing a one-time load into a temporary Splunk index from a file will ensure that any problems or incorrect field extractions won't cause dirty data to be loaded and stored with clean, tested data.

This is especially crucial when you know you will have to transform the data, for instance, using `props.conf` and `transforms.conf`. During that development process, there could be many different configurations that need to be tested and validated, so having an index where things can be tested and cleaned up without concern is a big help.

Searching within an index

Always remember to filter your searches by index. Not restricting your search to a specific index makes Splunk go through all available indexes, consuming unnecessary time and resources. The same can be said about filters for sourcetype if your searches only need to consider a specific set of data that resides in an index with many sourcetypes.

A normal question arises when designing your Splunk implementation about how many indexes to have and what data goes into each. Careful thought needs to be taken when planning for indexes and when you create a new index.

For example, all web server logs for the same software application can be placed in one index. You may then split the log types by sourcetype but keep them within the same index. This will give you a generally favorable search speed even if you have to search between two different source types.

Consider this example:

Index name	Source type
App1	Logs.Error
App1	Logs.Info
App1	Logs.Warning
App2	Logs.Error
App2	Logs.Info
App3	Logs.Warning

As you can see, we have indexed by app number first and then created various sourcetypes. You may then create a search within the same index, even if you have to combine two sourcetypes:

- A good search in this example:

      SPL> index=App1 sourcetype=Logs.Error OR Logs.Warning

- A bad search:

      SPL> sourcetype=Logs.* Error

The way we have set it up here, if you ever have to retrieve data from both indexes, you can combine them with the following query. It is not as efficient as searching against a single index, but it is better than going through all other available indexes:

    SPL> index=App1 OR index=App2 sourcetype=Logs.Error

Search within a limited time frame

By default, the **Search & Reporting** app's time range is set to **Last 24 hours**. Searches done using the **All Time** time frame will generally perform slower based on the volume and relative quantity of how much historical data is in the index. This problem grows when there are concurrent users doing the same thing. Although you can train your users to select a limited time range, not everybody will do this.

If you want to make the time range even shorter by default, you can simply change the default time range from the drop-down menu. We will do this by modifying the `ui-prefs.conf` file in an administrative Command Prompt.

Edit the following file:

> `SPLUNK_HOME/etc/system/local/ui-prefs.conf`

Copy and paste the following into the file:

```
[search]
dispatch.earliest_time = -4h
dispatch.latest_time = now
[default]
dispatch.earliest_time = -4h
dispatch.latest_time = now
```

Save the file and restart Splunk. Go back to the **Search & Reporting** app and the default time range should now say **Last 4 hours**. Note that this will also change the default time range in the Search dashboard of the **Destinations** app since any change in the default will be automatically applied to all apps, unless specified otherwise.

Quick searches via fast mode

There are three types of search modes in Splunk: **Fast Mode**, **Smart Mode**, and **Verbose Mode**:

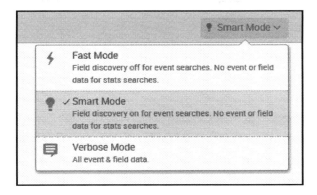

If you want your searches to be faster, use **Fast Mode**. Fast mode will not attempt to generate fields during search time, unlike the default smart mode. This is very good to use when you do not know what you are looking for. **Smart Mode** looks for transforming commands in your searches. If it finds these, it acts like fast mode; if it doesn't, then it acts like verbose mode. **Verbose Mode** means that the search will provide as much information as possible even though this may result in significantly slower searches.

Using event sampling

Like the fact that you only need a drop of blood to test for the amount of sugar and sodium levels in your blood, you often only need a small amount of data from large datasets to make conclusions to build accurate searches. When developing and testing in Splunk, event sampling can be particularly useful against large datasets:

Event sampling uses a sample ratio value that reduces the number of results. If a typical search result returns 1,000 events, a **1:10** event sampling ratio will return 100 events. As you can see from the previous screenshot, these ratios can significantly cut the amount of data searched, and can range from a fairly large ratio (which can be set using the **Custom...** setting) to one as small as **1:100,000** (or even smaller, again using the **Custom...** setting).

This is not suitable for searches for which you need accurate counts. This is, however, perfect when you are testing your searches as they will return significantly faster. Much of the time you will spend in Splunk is taken up with trying and retrying queries using SPL. If you have to deal with a large amount of data in each execution of a search, then your productivity will be negatively impacted. Consider using event sampling to reduce the time it takes to create useful searches.

The following steps indicate the steps you should take in this process:

- Do a quick search to ensure that the correct event data is present
- Look over the characteristics of the events and determine how you want to analyze them
- Set your event sampling for the level you find useful and efficient for this stage in the process
- Test your search commands against the resulting subset of data
- Keep going through this process until you have a search that you are happy with

When you are done, make sure to reset event sampling to **No Event Sampling** before saving your search query to a dashboard, otherwise the search will generate incomplete results.

Use the fields command to improve search performance

Traditionally when building a Splunk search, you will write the search first to get the correct layout and accurate results. Then using Splunk's fields command, the performance of the search can be improved, sometimes dramatically depending the logic contained in the search.

By default, when you search an index and return events, Splunk will query and return all of the event fields. However in most searches producing statistical results, having all the fields from the event is not necessary because they are not all required to create the output.

An example of a Splunk search before the fields command:

```
index=main http_uri=/booking/reservation http_status_code=200 | stats count
by http_user_agent
```

An example of the search after applying the fields command will produce the same results more quickly:

```
index=main http_uri=/booking/reservation http_status_code=200 | fields
http_user_agent | stats count by http_user_agent
```

In the case above, the only field returned from the search of the index is the http_user_agent field. No other event fields are unnecessarily captured and loaded into memory to produce the output due to the fields command. Using the fields command is a great way to improve searches after the results have been proven to be accurate.

Advanced searches

There are various kinds of advanced searches you may need as you plan out how to create searches and dashboards for your data. Consider the ones that we present, for they will help you design queries that are more efficient and cost effective.

Subsearch

A subsearch is a search within a search. If your main search requires data as a result of another search, use Splunk's subsearch capability to combine two searches into one.

Say you want to find statistics about the server that generates the most HTTP status 500 errors. You can achieve your goal of finding the culprit server with two searches.

The first search, shown next, will return the server address with the most 500 errors. Note that you are setting the limit to 1 and giving the instructions (using the + sign) to include just the server_ip field:

```
SPL> index=main http_status_code=500 | top limit=1 server_ip
     | fields + server_ip
```

The result of this code will be one of three IP addresses generated by from our Eventgen data.

In the following second search, the IP address filter is applied with the `server_ip` value from the first search result and delivers the top values of the `http_uri` and `client_ip` fields. In the second search, you are simply asking for the top `http_uri` and `client_ip` fields for data that has been piped through to that point, or the data from the indicated server with the top number of 500 codes:

```
SPL> index=main server_ip=10.2.1.34 | top http_uri, client_ip
```

You can combine these two searches into one using a subsearch. Note the subsearch appears within brackets:

```
SPL> index=main [ search index=main http_status_code=500
     | top limit=1 server_ip
     | fields + server_ip ] | top http_uri, client_ip
```

For example, consider a case where you have two or more indexes for various application logs. You can set up a search of these logs that will let you know what shared field has a value that is not in another index. An example of how you can do this is shown here:

```
SPL> sourcetype=a_sourcetype NOT [search sourcetype=b_sourcetype
     | fields field_val]
```

The default number of results is set to 100. This is because a subsearch with a large number of results will tend to slow down performance.

Using append

Once you have done a subsearch, you may want to add the results of that subsearch to another set of results. If that is the case, and you are using historical data, use the syntax provided here to append the subsearch:

```
SPL>   . . | append [subsearch]
```

You can also specify various timing options if you like.

Using join

People with experience in **Structured Query Language (SQL)** will be familiar with the concept of a join. You can use the `join` command to join the results of the subsearch to your main search results. As part of the `join` command, you will want to identify a field to join on. Again, the basic syntax is simple:

```
SPL> . . | join field_name [subsearch]
```

This will default to an inner join, which includes only events shared in common by the two searches. You can also specify an outer or left join. The outer join contains all the data from both searches, whereas the left join contains the data from events fulfilling main search, as well as the events that are shared in common.

Using eval and if

If you need to create a field for reporting, based on the data present in an event, you can use the `eval` command to create a field and use `if` to check for that condition.

The `eval` command takes the following form:

```
SPL> | eval newfield=if(condition, field1, field2)
```

Say you want to create two additional fields during search time to determine whether a destination is in the east coast or not. Using the following search, if a destination URI has NY, MIA, or MCO in it, a new field called East will be added to each of those events. Otherwise, Splunk will add a new field called Others. Once that has been done, this code will list the newly created Region field and http_uri for all events, and will sort by Region:

```
SPL> index=main http_uri="/destination/*/details"
     | eval Region=if(match(http_uri, "NY|MIA|MCO"), "East", "Others")
     | top 0 Region, http_uri | sort Region
```

A little regular expression has been used here to do a case statement between the airport codes: NY|MIA|MCO. If the http_uri includes NY, MIA, or MCO, then its Region field value will be East; otherwise, it will be Others.

This should now return the data with the new fields:

Region ⇕	http_uri ⇕
East	/destination/NY/details
East	/destination/MCO/details
East	/destination/MIA/details
Others	/destination/HOU/details
Others	/destination/WAS/details
Others	/destination/SEA/details
Others	/destination/PML/details
Others	/destination/AK/details
Others	/destination/LAX/details

(20 Per Page ∨   ✎Format ∨   Preview ∨)

Using eval and match with a case function

You can improve upon the prior search by using `match` instead of `if` and account for `West` and `Central`.

We also introduce the `case` function here. In the following illustration, you will see that we can set the value of a field by giving it a value of `Label1` if `Condition1` is `true`, `Label2` if `Condition2` is `true`, and so on:

```
SPL> | eval newfield=case(Condition1, "Label1", Condition2, Label2",
        ConditionX, "LabelX")
```

Let us tweak the previous query to use `case` instead of `if`:

```
SPL> index=main http_uri="/destination/*/details"
     | eval Region=case(match(http_uri, "NY|MIA|MCO"),
       "East", match(http_uri, "WAS|AK|LAX|PML"), "West",
       match(http_uri, "HOU"), "Central")
     | top 0 Region, http_uri | sort Region
```

The result will now properly classify the destinations based on the region:

Region ⇕	http_uri ⇕
Central	/destination/HOU/details
East	/destination/MCO/details
East	/destination/NY/details
East	/destination/MIA/details
West	/destination/WAS/details
West	/destination/LAX/details
West	/destination/PML/details
West	/destination/AK/details

20 Per Page ⌄   ✎Format ⌄   Preview ⌄

Summary

In this chapter, you learned some best practices to employ when using Splunk. You were also shown complex queries that can further enhance your result set.

9
Taking Splunk to the Organization

Throughout this book, we've been teaching you the fundamentals of using Splunk and building powerful analytics which can help an organization in a variety of ways. In this chapter, we will conclude our book with thoughts, concepts, and ideas to take this new knowledge ahead and apply to an organization.

Common organizational use cases

Most organizations will start using Splunk in one of three areas: IT operations management, information security, or **development operations (DevOps)**.

IT operations

IT operations have moved from predominantly being a cost center to also being a revenue center. Today, many of the world's oldest companies also make money based on IT services and/or systems. As a result, the delivery of these IT services must be monitored and, ideally, proactively remedied before failures occur. Ensuring that hardware such as servers, storage, and network devices are functioning properly via their log data is important. Organizations can also log and monitor mobile and browser-based software applications for any issues from software.

Ultimately, organizations will want to correlate these sets of data together to get a complete picture of IT Health. In this regard, Splunk takes the expertise accumulated over the years and offers a paid-for application known as **IT Server Intelligence (ITSI)** to help give companies a framework for tackling large IT environments.

Complicating matters for many traditional organizations is the use of Cloud computing technologies, which now drive log captured from both internally and externally hosted systems.

Cybersecurity

With the relentless focus in today's world on cybersecurity, there is a good chance your organization will need a tool such as Splunk to address a wide variety of Information Security needs as well. Splunk acts as a log data consolidation and reporting engine, capturing essential security-related log data from devices and software, such as vulnerability scanners, phishing prevention, firewalls, and user management and behavior, just to name a few. Companies need to ensure they are protected from external as well as internal threats, and as a result offer the paid-for applications enterprise security and **User behavior analytics** (**UBA**). Similar to ITSI, these applications deliver frameworks to help companies meet their specific requirements in these areas.

In addition to cyber-security to protect the business, often companies will have to comply with, and audit against, specific security standards, which can be industry-related, such as PCI compliance of financial transactions; customer-related, such as **National Institute of Standards and Technologies** (**NIST**) requirements in working with the the US government; or data privacy-related, such as the **Health Insurance Portability and Accountability Act** (**HIPAA**) or the European Union's **General Data Protection Regulation** (**GPDR**).

Software development and support operations

Commonly referred to as DevOps, Splunk's ability to ingest and correlate data from many sources solves many challenges faced in software development, testing, and release cycles. Using Splunk will help teams provide higher quality software more efficiently. Then, with the controls into the software in place, Splunk provides visibility into released software, its use and user behavior changes, intended or not. This set of use cases is particularly applicable to organizations that develop their own software.

Internet of Things

Many organizations today are looking to build upon the converging trends in computing, mobility and wireless communications and data to capture data from more and more devices. Examples can include data captured from sensors placed on machinery such as wind turbines, trains, sensors, heating, and cooling systems. These sensors provide access to the data they capture in standard formats such as **JavaScript Object Notation (JSON)** through **application programming interfaces (APIs)**.

Splunk architecture considerations

As an organization deploys Splunk, it will have specific requirements related to the architecture, its resiliency, and disaster recovery.

Splunk architecture for an organization

Usage, data volume, and criticality are the three biggest determinants of how much hardware you need in your Splunk environment. If you have large data volumes, a single server may not have enough processor capacity to index and provide searching together. Alternatively, consider the notion of installing Splunk on a single server. If that server were to fail, your Splunk application would fail along with it. If Splunk becomes a critical part of the organization, the cost of server failure may outweigh the costs of more hardware and set-up time to protect against failure.

Splunk provides the ability to configure a multi-tiered environment that can expand and load-balance search and usage activity, separate from indexing and storage activity.

Search capacity

When Splunk executes a search, all runtime search processing happens in the Splunk searching layer component known as a **search head**. When a Splunk search runs, it executes on a single CPU processor core by the search head, which then works with the various indexing resources to capture, summarize, and present the results. Therefore, the number of cores must be able to handle the amount of concurrent searching you users will require, which includes scheduled searches, ad hoc use, alerts, and so on. It is important to monitor these channels of search activity as usage of the Splunk environment increases. Consuming all search resources will deteriorate the user's experience. Monitoring growing demand and staying ahead of full capacity will be important.

Indexing capacity and data replication

Splunk provides the ability to cluster index servers together for high volume environments. Splunk also provides data replication services across the cluster nodes to survive a cluster node failure. A node in the index cluster is referred to as a peer. More than one peer will actively index data. A separate master node coordinates replication and supports search activity across the peers. Splunk training will provide guidelines for search and indexed data volume to help guide your hardware sizing activities.

High availability for critical environments

An independent factor driving a clustering approach is criticality of the application and its data. If there is high cost to not having Splunk and the data available, building a Splunk architecture for high availability ensures maximum uptime. In addition to search head and index clusters, load balancers, and storage backups should also be considered as external technologies critical to helping the Splunk environment be successful in highly critical situations.

Monitoring Console

Splunk administrators use the **Monitoring Console** delivered with Splunk Enterprise to monitor the health of their Splunk environment. As with all their products and components, Splunk provides nice documentation for the **Monitoring Console** as well. Documentation on the **Monitoring Console** can be found here: `http://docs.splunk.com/Documentation/Splunk/latest/DMC/DMCoverview`:

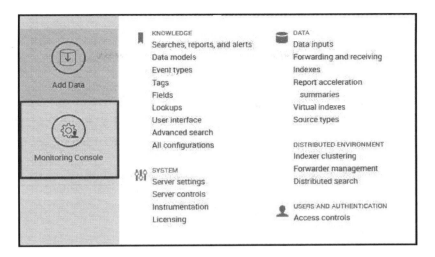

In the case of the **Monitoring Console**, the source of the data being shown is Splunk itself. Splunk is monitoring itself and providing important real time statistics on a variety of important topics. Some of the most commonly used areas of the **Monitoring Console** are:

- Search and indexing performance
- Operating system resource usage
- Index and volume usage
- Forwarder and TCP performance
- License usage

The hardware configuration used above is for demo purposes. Organizations will require more hardware resources to run Splunk based on data volume and search demands.

There is additional functionality in the **Monitoring Console** for monitoring the HTTP event collector and many other components of Splunk.

If your organization decides to use Splunk Cloud, you will still have access to the **Monitoring Console** to help you ensure that the Splunk environment you are paying for is working properly and license usage is appropriate for the amount of license capacity purchased.

Forwarders

Almost always found is organizational Splunk deployments are Splunk components called **forwarders**. A forwarder is a component of Splunk which is used to send data to another Splunk instance.

Within the forwarder arena, there are two kinds of forwarders which can be deployed, and since they offer different kinds of functionality, we will review them here.

Universal forwarder

A Splunk universal forwarder is a very small piece of Splunk software which resides on other machines and proactively sends data to downstream Splunk Enterprise components, most commonly for data indexing. A common example for the use of universal forwarders is for sending OS logs from either Windows or Linux servers to the central Splunk Enterprise instance, to monitor a variety of items.

Heavy forwarder

A Splunk heavy forwarder is a full Splunk Enterprise instance; however, some functionality is disabled. Different to the universal forwarder, a heavy forwarder parses data before forwarding it, which can be of help in complex data environments. A heavy forwarder can also direct data to different indexes in different locations, based on data contained with the event, such as the source IP address or kind of event. Since the heavy forwarder is almost a fully functional Splunk instance, it can index data locally, while also forwarding the data to another index peer.

Splunk Cloud

While most of the contents of this book focused on using Splunk, we spent the first chapter installing Splunk. If your organization would prefer not having to install and support its own Splunk environment, Splunk provides its **Software-as-a-Service (SaaS)** offering feature known as **Splunk Cloud**. The pricing is higher than regular Splunk because you compensate Splunk for using their hardware assets and their software administration. For example, when the newest release of Splunk inevitably comes out, the Splunk Cloud instances will be upgraded by Splunk, whereas if you had your own installation of Splunk, you would be forced to perform the upgrade. Inevitably, software environments installed on your own will fall behind the present release and at some point need to be upgrade by you or your Splunk administrator. Also consider that using Splunk does not absolve any local Splunk components. You will still need universal forwarders as well in your environment as Splunk recommends using a heavy forwarder to be a consolidation point for data locally, to then transfer to Splunk Cloud.

Splunk pricing model

Ultimately for an organization to use Splunk, it has to be bought for that organization. Briefly here, we will cover some of the important points to consider related to the purchase of software from Splunk.

The most important concept to understand is the concept of *Indexed Volume per Day*. Index volume per day represents the total of all the data you intend to send to Splunk on a daily basis. Any size license can be purchased over 1 GB per day, and over time the organization can purchase additional license capacity as new data sources are loaded into Splunk to support additional Splunk solutions.

After a license size estimate, the next decision to make is whether the organization intends to buy Splunk Cloud or buy Splunk to run and maintain on its own:

- Splunk Cloud is priced on a monthly basis, but billed annually. Meaning, if you buy an annual license, the price quoted could be $150 per month, but the invoice you receive to pay will be for 12 months or $1,800. We will refer to this way to buy software as **Term**.
- Splunk Enterprise bought to be captured, installed and maintained by the organization can be bought in one of two ways:
    - **Term**: The same method as discussed above for Splunk Cloud
    - **Perpetual**: Take ownership of software with a higher up front cost and lower annual costs after 1 year.

The main difference is in perpetual, the organization takes ownership of the software to do as they so chose, for a higher up front cost. In the case of term, if the organization decides after 1 year to not purchase another year for 2 year, they lose access to the software and all its contents.

Splunk provides a good deal of information on how it prices its software on its website here: `https://www.splunk.com/en_us/products/pricing.html`. There is also a helpful page of frequently asked questions to review: `https://www.splunk.com/en_us/products/pricing/faqs.html`.

Commonly in software, there is also a cost for what as known as **support**. Support generally covers the ability to work with Splunk on product issues you may encounter as well as the rights to use new releases of software in your environments as they are delivered to the market. Depending on which type of license you buy, support will be bundled into the cost of the software or listed as a separate item, as is the case with perpetual licenses.

To close the topic of Splunk pricing, there are a few important things to understand about Splunk software which you can do for free:

- Deploy to unlimited amount of users – no cost per user
- Deploy to an unlimited amount of hardware resources – increase performance and resiliency without additional software cost
- Collect data from an unlimited number of sources
- There is no cost to deploy universal forwarders where needed

The Splunk community and online resources

When considering software for organizational purposes, it is important in today's world to consider online presence and community. Is the community very closed with little community fanfare or is it more open with significant online resources, documentation, and other community-based assets.

In addition to the great product, Splunk is also successful because it has a strong online community which is built, in large part, to help customers successfully implement the product for their needs.

The Splunk online community site can be a good starting point to help you tap into the following resources (`https://www.splunk.com/en_us/community.html`):

- **SplunkBase**: `splunkbase.splunk.com` provides Splunk apps and add-ons for you to consider based on your needs, as well as the sources of data in your organization. Premium Splunk-built apps such as ITSI and ES can be found here. Free Splunk-built apps can also be found here. Free apps like security essentials can provide good value. Common IT vendors such as Amazon Web Services, Cisco, Microsoft, ServiceNow, and many others may provide add-ons, as well as apps, to help you source and load their data into Splunk. The apps contain prebuilt reports, dashboards, and models to get analytical value from the data once loaded. We highly recommend leveraging the assets on SplunkBase to help you realize the value in Splunk fast.

- **Splunk Answers**: `answers.splunk.com` is an online forum where people implementing Splunk can present questions to the community and responses can be provided. As you learn Splunk, you should know that many of the challenges and problems you will no doubt overcome have likely already been remedied by someone else, somewhere else.

- **Splunk Docs**: `docs.splunk.com` is the gateway to all official Splunk documentation for all current and recent prior releases of Splunk, apps and other artifacts. Be sure to use the right documentation for the right version of Splunk being implemented. Functionality improvements made of time to Splunk may not be available in older releases.

- **Splunk for Developers**: `dev.splunk.com` contains specific information for software developers who are looking to write add-ons and applications leveraging the Splunk platform. It also has content for software developers who want to integrate with the Splunk platform using REST API's, software development kits and developer tools, such as Splunk plugins for the eclipse integrated development environment and Visual Studio for .NET.

- **Blogs**: Splunk routinely posts in one of their many blog categories focused on common topics. Here is a short list of blog categories:
    - **Security**: `https://www.splunk.com/blog/category/security.html`
    - **Machine learning**: `https://www.splunk.com/blog/category/machine-learning.html`
    - **Customers**: `https://www.splunk.com/blog/category/customers.html`
    - **Tips and tricks**: `https://www.splunk.com/blog/category/tips-and-tricks.html`

- **Education**: It is hard to be very successful quickly with Splunk without some educational help. There are a variety of training tracks available based on user and system needs.
- **Slack**: There is a Splunk community available using this popular messaging application.

Summary

In this chapter, we saw how Splunk can be used at an organizational level for IT operations, cybersecurity, software development and support and the IoTs. We reviewed critical topics related to the planning of your Splunk infrastructure, including forwarders. We provided details for acquiring Splunk software through purchase and provided insights into the vast set of resources available through the Splunk online community.

We have enjoyed taking you through the first step in a very rewarding journey to use Splunk to benefit yourself or organization. You now have the skills and insights you need to take the product, explore its abilities with your data and build upon initial successes you may have.

Index

Made in the USA
San Bernardino, CA
17 September 2018